the Southern Bite

COOKBOOK

the Southern Bite

COOKBOOK

MORE THAN 150 IRRESISTIBLE
DISHES FROM 4 GENERATIONS
OF MY FAMILY'S KITCHEN

STACEY LITTLE

PHOTOGRAPHY BY KIM BOX

NELSON
BOOKS

An Imprint of Thomas Nelson

Published in Nashville, Tennessee, by Nelson Books, an imprint of Thomas Nelson. Nelson Books and Thomas Nelson are registered trademarks of HarperCollins Christian Publishing, Inc.

DR PEPPER is a registered trademark of Dr Pepper/Seven Up, Inc.

Photography by Kim Box

Thomas Nelson, Inc., titles may be purchased in bulk for educational, business, fund-raising, or sales promotional use. For information, please e-mail SpecialMarkets@ThomasNelson.com.

Library of Congress Cataloging-in-Publication Data

Little, Stacey, 1981–
  The Southern bite cookbook : more than 150 irresistible dishes from 4 generations of my family's kitchen / Stacey Little.
      pages cm
   Includes index.
   ISBN 978-1-4016-0543-8
1. Cooking, American—Southern style. I. Title.
   TX715.2.S68L577 2014
   641.5975—dc23   2013032371

Printed in the United States of America

14 15 16 17 QG 6 5 4 3

To my mother, who taught me that any food, no matter how basic or inexpensive, made with love is the best food.

Contents

FOREWORD

HERE IN THE SOUTH, IT'S ALL ABOUT FAMILY. FAMILY GET-togethers, family memories, and family recipes dominate our social landscape, and that's just how we like it. As a result, we tend to have an extended family network everywhere we go and share many of the same traditions and even foods.

That's where this wonderful cookbook comes in.

The beautiful thing about sitting down with a cookbook is that you're not just curling up with words on paper, bound together. You're sitting down to visit and get to know the author. As the old Southern invitation goes, "Sit a spell; stay awhile." A cookbook invites you to come into our lives and to allow us to linger in yours. So it's important when choosing one that it's written by someone you know you're gonna like spending time with—someone who feels like family.

When I first met Stacey, he came to one of my book signings, but he stood out. While some were checking their watches and looking at the line, Stacey was grinning from ear to ear, making friends with everyone around him, and holding a big old plate of Pecan Chewies! The moment he introduced himself, there was a connection. Sometimes when you meet someone, you realize they're more than a friend—they're family. It was as if God had made us from the same speck of dust and he was my long-lost brother from heaven. We became fast friends, and he's been part of my family ever since.

I love Stacey's attitude toward life, his heart for others, and anything that comes out of his kitchen is sure to set stomachs to growling!

Family is a precious thing, and I'm of the mind that you can never have too many precious things in your life. So I am glad to see you inviting Stacey into yours. You won't regret it.

The recipes in this book are the best kind of food: simple, straightforward, and delicious. These are recipes from four generations of Stacey's family, and I can tell you from personal experience, each generation I've had the honor of meeting has been as good as gold.

So from my adopted brother's family to yours, sit a spell and stay awhile. It tastes just like home here.

Christy Jordan
Author of *Southern Plate*

INTRODUCTION

I'M NOT A CHEF. I'VE NEVER CLAIMED TO BE ONE. I HAVE NO FORMAL culinary training, and that's fine with me. My practical kitchen knowledge comes from being under the feet of my mother, grandmother, and great-grandmother as they prepared meals for our family. From the time I was old enough to hold a spoon, I've found that the kitchen holds a sense of comfort for me like no other place. Some of my earliest memories are sitting on the floor of my grandparents' kitchen, pulling out all of my grandmother's pots, pans, bowls, and spoons, and cooking up a storm. The kitchen is my place to be. I never grow tired of the comfort it provides me.

Who am I, and why should you listen to me? The truth is, I'm not sure. I've been blessed to live a rather uneventful life. I have no fancy title or special abbreviations after my name. My designations are more like daddy, husband, son, and friend. And though some strive for acclaim, celebrity, and wealth, I'm perfectly happy with the titles I already have. My struggles each day are about my being the best daddy, husband, son, and friend I can be. I'm human, though, so most days are put to bed with thoughts that I could have done a little better or tried a little harder. To put it simply, every day I pray that God will bless me with the wisdom to be a better person than I was the day before. It might sound simple, but it's how I live my life.

My mother taught me years ago that being positive is the key to so many of life's successes. I wake up each morning with the realization that regardless of what happens to throw my day off track, I have the ability to make it a good day or a bad one. It's my choice whether to allow the negative things that might happen to have such an influence over me that they ruin my day. I use that philosophy in my entire life too. My journey hasn't always been easy, but not a year goes by that we all don't face challenges and hardships. It's how we allow those negatives to influence us and shape our lives that really matters. We can allow those bad things to define us and control us, or we can allow them to make us better people.

I never set out to write a cookbook. But one thing that I've learned in this process is that I have a lot to say—about food, that is. Food and family are two of the most important things in my life. When I write about my family and the food that has defined us for generations, I can write volumes.

I was fortunate to grow up in a household where my mother cooked three meals a day. Every evening found us all gathered at the kitchen table for supper. I've discovered that rarely do families gather around the table like that to share a meal anymore. Our fast-paced lives seldom allow time for a home-cooked meal, and when they do, those meals are often interrupted by e-mails, texts, and phone calls. Our families, our culture, need to get back to uninterrupted mealtimes together.

I have the great fortune of being presented with a unique opportunity, one that many folks can only dream of. Through these pages, I get to share my passion with you—my food. That food is a patchwork of the amazing cooks that came before me. It's a collection of time-honored recipes that have been updated, honed, and perfected through the years. Now, you won't find me going on against the use of convenience products like cream of chicken soup and instant brown gravy mix. I think for most folks, getting dinner on the table is challenge enough, and I don't know about you, but I'll be glad to take all the help I can get. I'm sure there are healthier alternatives to things like ranch dressing and onion soup mixes, but my philosophy is that the relationships we develop around the table sharing a meal as a family are far more important than any cream of chicken soup.

Five years ago I started a little blog. *Southern Bite* was a creative space for me to share my restaurant reviews and musings. After a get-together where several folks requested one of my recipes, I decided to add the recipe to the blog and send them a link. The recipe quickly became the most popular thing on the blog, and as they say, "The rest is history." Today the blog has little resemblance to what it once was. The evolution of *Southern Bite* has helped me understand the importance of capturing and preserving the recipes of my family. It has become one of my life's missions to document the recipes that have been passed down through the generations. Many of them have never been written down until now. Adding those recipes to the blog and now to a book allows me to share my family's food with the world.

Each day I receive comments on the blog that offer praise (and sometimes criticism) of my recipes and stories, but one comment has stayed with me like no other. It was a simple sentence that has sculpted and molded the way I've blogged each day since: "I love your blog because I feel like you're just sitting across the kitchen table from me and we're just chatting." I hope that you find this book to be just that—a friendly chat, a friend passing along a great recipe. That, in itself, is my ultimate goal—to share my recipes with you. I realize that we are all pulled in so many different directions, especially around supper time, so I've done my best to make these recipes approachable, with the fewest ingredients and the most flavor.

I imagine that this book will be different things to different people. For some, it will be merely another bound collection of recipes sitting on a dusty shelf. I'm thrilled just at the thought that my name might be alongside some of the folks who have my utmost admiration. To others, though, I hope this book might be a connection to their past—to their mother or grandmother. Many of these recipes are generations older than I am. I'm just the lucky one who gets to share them with you.

One of the things that makes me the most proud about this book is the inclusion of some of my faithful readers' family recipes. Without the amazing folks who find their way back to SouthernBite.com each week, I would have never been offered the unbelievable opportunity to write this book. So it is for their love, loyalty, support, and friendship that I will be forever grateful. This is *our* book. It's not just my work; it's the collective work of the folks who came before me, the readers who have submitted recipes, and the folks who came before them too.

Thank you for cracking the spine of this book to take a gander. Without knowing, you've just become a big part of this humble Alabama boy's dream come true. I've always dreamed of sharing my food with the world, and you just let me do that. So from me, my mom, my Nana, and my Big Mama . . . y'all enjoy!

Stacey's Kitchen Tips

- Bacon grease is the rendered fat left over after cooking bacon. No true Southern kitchen is complete without it stowed away. We use it for all kinds of things, but especially to season vegetables. Though there are many schools of thought in terms of storing the stuff, I store mine in an airtight container in the refrigerator for about a month—if it lasts that long.

- To make your own self-rising flour, sift together 1 1/2 teaspoons of baking powder, 1/2 teaspoon of salt, and 1 cup of all-purpose flour for each cup of self-rising flour needed.

- Out of buttermilk? Simply stir together 1 tablespoon of white vinegar or lemon juice with 1 cup of whole milk. Allow it to sit for about 10 minutes before using.

- Make your own light brown sugar by combining 1 tablespoon of molasses with 1 cup of granulated sugar. Add 2 tablespoons of molasses for dark brown sugar.

- When a recipe calls for shredded or chopped cooked chicken, as many of mine do, feel free to use the meat from a grocery store rotisserie chicken. But if you're going to cook the chicken yourself, resist the temptation to throw a few frozen chicken breasts into boiling water. The chicken should be completely thawed and will be much more tender if you cook it as low and slow as possible. I learned this the hard way.

- The difference between a tablespoon of table salt and a tablespoon of kosher salt can make or break a dish. Every recipe in this book uses plain table salt out of a cardboard dispenser.

Party Bites

In the South, we love a good party and know how to do them up right. I mean, we're credited for creating America's modern Mardi Gras celebration, and there's a lot to be said for that. We celebrate everything down here—birthdays, engagements, babies, anniversaries, job promotions, going-aways, you name it. We have festivals that honor everything from okra to cornbread and from grits to the chicken and the egg (yes, there really is a chicken and egg festival). The common thread that runs through all these events and celebrations is food.

Whether it's a backyard barbecue or a black-tie affair, we Southerners love to put out a spread that rivals any fancy Las Vegas buffet. I've always said that cooking is one of the ways a Southerner shows love to someone. It might be as simple as a pound cake or a covered-dish casserole, but it can speak volumes. We use food to celebrate, to say thanks, as an apology, or just to say, "I love you."

BACON AND CREAM CHEESE STUFFED MUSHROOMS

My wife, who doesn't like mushrooms, loves these. I mean, even if you don't like mushrooms, surely you're a bacon and cream cheese fan. Right? Regardless, these are a great easy appetizer that will impress your family and your guests.

6 slices bacon

1 pound button mushrooms

4 ounces cream cheese, softened

1/2 teaspoon garlic powder

1/2 teaspoon onion powder

1/2 cup grated Parmesan cheese

Preheat the oven to 350°. Lightly grease a jelly-roll pan.

In a large skillet cook the bacon over medium heat until crispy. While the bacon cooks, use a clean dish towel to wipe the mushrooms clean. Remove the stems and coarsely chop them. Place the caps on the baking sheet.

Once the bacon is crispy, drain it on paper towels and then crumble it. Pour away all but 2 tablespoons of the remaining bacon grease.

Return the skillet with the remaining bacon grease to the heat. Add the chopped mushroom stems and cook until they are tender. Pour the cooked mushroom stems into a large bowl, and add the crumbled bacon, cream cheese, garlic powder, onion powder, and Parmesan cheese. Stir gently to combine. Spoon about 1 tablespoon of the filling into each of the mushroom caps. Bake 18 to 20 minutes or until the filling is heated through.

Makes about 20 mushrooms

There isn't a proper Southern social event that doesn't have sausage balls on the menu. These things show up at birthday parties, bridal and baby showers, wedding receptions, and of course, the holidays—just to name a few. Feel free to use spicy sausage if that's more your speed.

Preheat the oven to 350°. In a large bowl combine the sausage, cheese, and baking mix. Gradually add water until the dough reaches the right consistency to handle. Roll into balls about 1 inch in size, and place on an ungreased baking sheet. Bake 10 to 12 minutes or until golden brown.

Makes about 3 dozen

1 pound ground sausage

3 cups shredded Cheddar cheese

2 cups baking mix

3 tablespoons water

This is one of those things that will probably make you say, "Hmm, I wonder if that's really any good." I can tell you it is. If you love fried pickles and fried okra, this is the best of both worlds. Trust me. It's good. Take a walk on the wild side.

Pour about 1 inch of oil into the bottom of a deep skillet or Dutch oven. Heat the oil over medium-high heat until it reaches about 350°.

In a small bowl lightly beat the eggs with the water. In a medium bowl combine the cornmeal, flour, salt, and pepper.

Slice each okra pod in half lengthwise, dip it into the egg wash, and then coat it in the dry mixture. Fry the coated okra for 4 to 6 minutes or until it is golden brown. Drain on paper towels.

Serve with ranch dressing as a dip.

Serves 4 to 6

Vegetable oil for frying

2 large eggs

2 tablespoons water

1 cup cornmeal

1/3 cup all-purpose flour

1/2 teaspoon salt

1/4 teaspoon black pepper

1 (16-ounce) jar pickled okra, drained

Ranch dressing for dipping

Pizza Pull-Apart Bread

This recipe might imply that there's something wrong with regular pizza and that it needed improving upon. Don't get me wrong; I love me some pizza. Sometimes it's just nice to dump everything in a bowl and stir, and that's what this is: dump, stir, bake, eat.

2 (16.3-ounce) cans large Southern-style biscuits

1 (14.5-ounce) jar pizza sauce

1/2 green bell pepper, seeded and diced

1/2 onion, finely diced

1/4 cup grated Parmesan cheese

1 (2.25-ounce) can sliced black olives, drained

1 (3-ounce) package pepperoni, coarsely chopped

2 cups mozzarella cheese, divided

Preheat the oven to 350°. Grease a Bundt or tube pan.

Cut each biscuit into quarters. In a large bowl combine the biscuits, sauce, bell pepper, onion, Parmesan cheese, olives, pepperoni, and 1 cup mozzarella cheese. Stir gently to combine, ensuring the biscuits are coated with sauce. Pour the mixture into the Bundt or tube pan, and bake 45 to 50 minutes or until the biscuits are golden brown and done throughout.

Remove from the oven and invert onto a platter while hot. Top with the remaining cup of mozzarella cheese.

Serves 8 to 10

Dill pickles are one of my favorite snacks. No burger or sandwich is complete without them at my house. This easy dip combines all the great flavors of a crisp dill pickle and is great served with chips or even with vegetables.

In a medium bowl combine the pickles, cream cheese, garlic powder, and salt. Add the pickle juice gradually to get the mixture to dipping consistency. Refrigerate for at least 30 minutes, and then serve chilled alongside crackers, potato chips, or vegetables.

Makes about 2 cups

1 1/2 cups finely diced kosher dill pickles

1 (8-ounce) package cream cheese, softened

1/4 teaspoon garlic powder

1/4 teaspoon salt

2 to 4 tablespoons pickle juice

Crackers, potato chips, or vegetables for serving

Ranch Cheese Ball

When my wife was getting her master's degree, she would use this cheese ball as a bargaining tool when she needed help studying. Apparently it was a pretty powerful offering—she graduated magna cum laude. If you like, you can skip molding it into a ball and place the mixture into a dish or bowl and use it as a dip.

2 (8-ounce) packages cream cheese, softened

1 (10-ounce) can white meat chicken, drained

1 (1-ounce) package ranch salad dressing mix

1/2 cup mayonnaise

1/2 cup finely shredded Cheddar cheese

1 cup chopped pecans

Crackers or vegetables for serving

In a medium bowl combine the cream cheese, chicken, ranch dressing mix, mayonnaise, and Cheddar cheese until thoroughly mixed. Chill for at least 2 hours.

Remove the mixture from the refrigerator, and mold it into a ball shape. Coat the outside with chopped pecans. Serve with assorted crackers or vegetables.

Serves 8 to 10

Slow Cooker Party Mix

DONYA MULLINS
GREENSBORO, NORTH CAROLINA

This recipe is from one of my blogger friends, Donya. She took the standard recipe for a party mix and adapted it for the slow cooker to save a little time. This method frees you up if you're scrambling last minute to get things ready for a party or get-together.

Melt the butter in a medium saucepan over low heat. Add the Worcestershire sauce, garlic salt, onion salt, and celery salt. Stir well.

Add the cereals, pretzels, and nuts to the bowl of a large slow cooker. Pour the butter mixture over the cereal mixture and gently mix until it is all coated. Cover the slow cooker and cook on low for 2 hours.

Remove the lid and stir. Cook uncovered for an additional 45 minutes, stirring every 10 to 15 minutes. Remove from the slow cooker, and allow to cool.

Serves about 15

1 ½ cups (3 sticks) butter

4 tablespoons Worcestershire sauce

1 tablespoon garlic salt

1 tablespoon onion salt

1 tablespoon celery salt

1 (14-ounce) box toasted oat cereal

1 (12.8-ounce) box square rice cereal

½ (14-ounce) box square wheat cereal

3/4 (16-ounce) bag small classic pretzels

2 (10.3-ounce) cans mixed nuts

PIMENTO CHEESE

This is another one of those Southern social staples. Every Southern cook worth his salt has a tried and true pimento cheese recipe. The addition of cream cheese in mine gives it a creamy texture that my family really enjoys. The key to this recipe is to grate your own cheese. The preshredded, bagged stuff is convenient, but it just doesn't work in this recipe. Plus, I'm giving you an opportunity to work on those biceps.

1 pound block sharp Cheddar cheese

4 ounces cream cheese, softened

½ cup mayonnaise

~~1 (4-ounce) jar chopped pimentos, well drained~~ *Cooked crumbled Bacon*

~~2 tablespoons grated onion~~

⅛ teaspoon freshly ground black pepper

1 teaspoon garlic powder

Salt

Shred the Cheddar cheese using a box grater. In a large bowl combine the shredded Cheddar, cream cheese, mayonnaise, pimentos, grated onion, pepper, and garlic powder. Stir until the mixture is combined. Add salt to taste. Refrigerate for at least a few hours, but preferably overnight to allow the flavors to blend.

Makes about 5 cups

This recipe is special because it comes from my best friend's grandmother. Laura and her family are so important to us. It's really an honor to be able to share a recipe that has been passed down through her family. We served this at Laura's birthday party a little while back, and it was a huge hit.

Combine the water, drink mix, and sugar in a large punch bowl, and mix well. Add the orange juice concentrate and lemon juice. Gently pour the lemon-lime soda into the punch, and stir to combine.

Makes 1 ½ gallons

16 cups cold (1 gallon) water

4 (0.13-ounce) cherry-flavored drink mix powder

2 cups sugar

1 (12-ounce) can frozen orange juice concentrate

Juice of 1 lemon

1 liter lemon-lime soda, chilled

What can you say about chicken salad other than everybody has their own recipe? This is my version that includes my favorite nut, the pecan. Whether you say pea-can or puh-kahn (or however else you might pronounce it), this nut adds a great flavor and crunch to the salad.

In a large bowl stir together the pickle relish, mustard, and mayonnaise. Add the chicken, eggs, celery, onion, and pecans. Stir to combine. Add salt and pepper to taste. Serve alongside crackers or toasted pita chips or in small tea sandwiches.

Makes about 6 cups

2 tablespoons pickle relish

2 teaspoons Creole mustard

1/2 cup mayonnaise

4 cups cooked chopped chicken

2 large hard-boiled eggs, finely chopped

2 ribs celery, finely chopped

1/4 medium onion, finely chopped

1/2 cup pecans, chopped

Salt and black pepper

Want even more nutty flavor? Toast the pecans in a 350° oven for 5 to 7 minutes or just until you can start to smell them. Cool them, and then add to the salad.

This is a fun Southern twist on the popular spinach dip. Even if you don't like turnip greens, I bet you'll like this. We enjoy it with tortilla chips, but also sometimes serve it with fried pork skins. Either way, it's always a favorite at our family gatherings.

6 slices bacon

1/2 large yellow onion, diced

1 (16-ounce) package frozen chopped turnip greens, thawed and drained

1 (15-ounce) jar prepared Alfredo sauce

1 (8-ounce) package cream cheese, cubed

1/2 teaspoon salt

1/4 teaspoon black pepper

1/2 teaspoon garlic powder

1/3 cup grated Parmesan cheese

Tortilla chips or fried pork skins for serving

Preheat the oven to 350°. Grease a 2-quart baking dish.

In a large skillet cook the bacon over medium heat until crispy. Remove the bacon, drain on paper towels, and crumble. Carefully pour away all but about 2 tablespoons of the bacon grease; return the pan to the heat, and add the onions. Cook about 3 minutes. Add the turnip greens and cook 8 to 10 minutes. Add the Alfredo sauce, cream cheese, salt, pepper, and garlic powder. Cook until the cream cheese has melted and the mixture is bubbly. Stir in the crumbled bacon.

Transfer the mixture to the baking dish, and bake 25 minutes. Remove from the oven and sprinkle with Parmesan cheese. Turn on the oven's broiler, and return the baking dish to the oven for 5 minutes. Serve with tortilla chips or fried pork skins.

Makes 6 cups

For me, the only things that are more Southern than fried green tomatoes are grits and fried okra. I love this recipe by itself, but I also love to replace the T in a BLT with an FGT. (Translation: make a bacon, lettuce, and tomato sandwich with fried green tomatoes instead of the fresh red variety.)

In a small bowl combine the mayonnaise, sour cream, ketchup, mustard, lemon juice, garlic, horseradish, and Creole seasoning. Stir well to combine. Refrigerate for at least 30 minutes to allow the flavors to develop.

Thinly slice the tomatoes, and lightly salt each side. Place in a colander in the sink and allow the salt to draw some of the moisture out.

In a medium bowl whisk the egg and buttermilk together. In another shallow bowl combine the cornmeal, flour, and pepper. In a deep skillet or Dutch oven, pour about 1 inch of oil into the bottom. Heat the oil over medium-high heat until the oil reaches about 350°.

Dip the tomatoes in the egg wash, and then dredge them in the cornmeal mixture, pressing lightly to coat them. Fry in the hot oil for 4 to 5 minutes on each side, or until golden brown. Drain on paper towels. Serve with the rémoulade sauce.

Serves 4 to 6

FOR THE RÉMOULADE:

1/2 cup mayonnaise

1/2 cup sour cream

2 tablespoons ketchup

2 tablespoons Creole or spicy brown mustard

1 tablespoon fresh lemon juice

2 garlic cloves, minced

2 teaspoons prepared horseradish

1/2 teaspoon Creole seasoning

FOR THE TOMATOES:

3 green tomatoes

Salt

1 large egg

1/2 cup buttermilk

3/4 cup cornmeal

1/2 cup all-purpose flour

1/2 teaspoon black pepper

vegetable oil for frying

all the same proportions

Leave it to a Southerner to go and try to improve upon pimento cheese. I humbly submit my Pimento Cheese Crisps. This is the ideal combination of pimento cheese and a cheese straw, and is perfect for any special occasion or even just for an everyday snack.

Pour the pimentos into a fine-mesh strainer, rinse, and drain very well. Using a box grater, grate the Cheddar cheese. In a large bowl combine the pimentos, cheese, butter, salt, garlic powder, red pepper, and flour. Stir until the ingredients are combined, then work with your hands until a thick dough forms. Turn the dough out onto a sheet of wax paper and form into a log. Roll the dough up in the wax paper and refrigerate for at least 1 hour.

Preheat the oven to 350°. Line a baking sheet with parchment paper. Slice the chilled dough into 1/8-inch thick rounds. Place the rounds on the baking sheet, and bake them for 12 to 14 minutes or until the edges just begin to brown. Cool on a wire rack. Work in batches until all the dough has been cooked.

Makes about 4 dozen

1 (4-ounce) jar diced pimentos

1 (8-ounce) block cheddar cheese

3/4 cup (1 1/2 sticks) butter, softened

1 1/2 teaspoons salt

1/2 teaspoon garlic powder

1/2 teaspoon ground red pepper (or more to taste)

2 cups all-purpose flour

You know that really famous movie where the guy is talking about all the ways that you can prepare shrimp? Well, other than fried, this is one of my favorite ways to make it. The addition of the avocado gives it a great creamy texture that I love with shrimp.

2 pounds medium shrimp, peeled, deveined, and cooked

1/2 cup diced celery

1/3 cup diced onion

1/2 cup mayonnaise

1 teaspoon seafood seasoning

2 tablespoons fresh lemon juice

1 avocado, diced

In a large bowl combine the cooked shrimp, celery, onions, mayonnaise, seafood seasoning, lemon juice, and avocado. Stir well, cover, and refrigerate for at least 1 hour to allow the flavors to develop. Serve the salad on a bed of lettuce with crackers or as a sandwich.

Serves 4 to 6

Buffalo Chicken Cheese Ball

MARGARET EICHLER
INDIANAPOLIS, INDIANA

Margaret was tired of the same old baked buffalo chicken dip she was used to. She and her daughter collaborated to create this yummy version that is more cheese-ball-like. She says it is great served with celery sticks.

In a medium saucepan over medium-low heat, stir together the chicken and wing sauce, breaking up the larger pieces of chicken. Add the cream cheese and sour cream. Stir to combine. Add the Cheddar cheese, and stir until it melts. Remove from the heat and allow the mixture to cool to room temperature. Once the mixture has cooled, add the blue cheese. Form the mixture into a ball, and roll it in the almonds. Serve at room temperature with various vegetables and crackers.

Serves 8 to 10

1 (12-ounce) can white meat chicken, drained

3/4 cup buffalo wing sauce

1 (8-ounce) package cream cheese, softened

1/2 cup sour cream

1 cup shredded sharp Cheddar cheese

1/2 cup blue cheese crumbles

1 cup slivered almonds

Assorted vegetables and crackers for serving

TWO-INGREDIENT PEPPER JELLY

Sure, you can go and buy a jar of pepper jelly, but where is your sport and spirit? In this one, you control the heat by adding more or less jalapeño. Plus, you get the chance to tell everyone you made it and no one will know that it has only two ingredients.

2 to 3 jalapeño peppers

1 (16-ounce) jar apple jelly

Seed and finely chop the jalapeños. In a medium saucepan combine the jelly and chopped peppers. Heat over medium until the jelly melts, stirring occasionally. Carefully return the hot mixture to the jar, replace the cap, and chill overnight, shaking occasionally to redistribute the peppers in the jelly. Keep refrigerated, and use within a week. Serve over a block of cream cheese alongside crackers.

Serves 8 to 10

Note: When handling hot peppers, be sure to wear gloves or wash your hands thoroughly after working with them. It's also a good idea to use a plastic cutting board or one made with another nonporous material.

DEVILED HAM

I have such fond childhood memories of a deviled ham sandwich, smeared with mayonnaise, on gummy white loaf bread. I'm not sure if we ate so many of them because they were good or because that's all we could afford. Either way, one bite of a deviled ham sandwich, and I can feel myself peering over the dusty blue countertops in my mom's kitchen, watching as she cuts my favorite sandwich into triangles.

In a food processor or food chopper, pulse the diced ham until finely minced. In a large bowl stir together the ham, mayonnaise, mustard, hot sauce, Worcestershire sauce, and vinegar, until combined. Refrigerate for at least 2 hours for best texture and flavor.

Serves about 4

- 1 1/2 pounds (about 4 cups) diced ham
- 3/4 cup mayonnaise
- 1 tablespoon Dijon mustard
- 1/4 teaspoon hot sauce
- 1 tablespoon Worcestershire sauce
- 1/2 teaspoon white vinegar

Skip the powdery mix, and make lemonade the old-fashioned way—by squeezing eight lemons. No, seriously, if you've never made homemade lemonade for your family, you should. There's just nothing quite like it. My son is five now and still asks for lemon-lade. I hope he still says it like that when he's forty.

7 cups water, divided

1 1/2 cups sugar

1 1/2 cups freshly squeezed lemon juice (about 8 lemons)

Make a simple syrup by combining 1 cup water with the sugar in a medium saucepan. Bring to a boil over medium-high heat, stirring occasionally. Remove the syrup from the heat, and allow it to cool to room temperature. In a large pitcher combine the simple syrup, 6 cups water, and the lemon juice. Stir to mix. Serve over ice.

Makes about 2 quarts

Note: Planning for a big party and need a little extra time? The simple syrup can be made several days in advance and stored in the refrigerator.

A Wooden Spoon Perspective

I'LL ADMIT THAT I WAS BORN WITH THE PROVERBIAL "SPOON IN MY mouth," but it wasn't what you'd expect. Silver was out of our price range. In fact, lots of things were out of our price range. My beginning was a humble one, to say the least. I was born to a twenty-one-year-old single mother who lived with her parents. To their credit, my parents were getting married, but when my biological father found out he was going to be a daddy, he left. While I'm sure it was traumatic for my mother to know she would be raising a child by herself, I can say that I'm positive that was one of the best decisions he ever made, at least for me.

When I was three, my mother married the man I call Dad. I may not have been his blood, but he was more of a father than I could ever have asked for. Looking back on the sacrifices he made for us, I'm not sure I'm man enough to have made those decisions myself. He worked long days and odd jobs at night and on the weekends just to make ends meet. Times were tough and money was nearly nonexistent, but we had a love that made us rich—rich in all the ways that really mattered.

While most folks would make every effort to hide or disguise their humble beginnings, mine is one of the things I'm most proud of. The funny thing is, when you grow up having to make do with just a little, you develop a sense of perspective that folks who are born into riches don't have. Coming from nothing really makes you appreciate things. The truth is you're poor only if you choose to be. For while we didn't have lots of money, fancy cars, or a big house, we did have something some folks can only dream of: we had a love that no amount of money could ever buy.

Today I'm fortunate to be raising my son in a lifestyle that has him wanting for little. And while he may not grow up with the same respect for material things that I have, I know that he will have all the love that one person can handle.

No, the spoon I was born with wasn't made of silver; it was a wooden one. And the perspective it has given me is worth more than all the riches in the world.

WEEKNIGHT BITES

IT SEEMS AS THOUGH OUR LIVES ARE GETTING BUSIER AND BUSIER. We're rushing from one place to another—work to school, school to the grocery store, the grocery store to home, home to the ball field or dance class. The result is that there is less and less time to get a decent meal on the table for our families. I've always believed that it's important for families to gather for supper every night. There's something about that opportunity to chat about your day that helps develop the bonds that families share. Having grown up in a household where we had supper together every night, I'll admit I'm a bit partial, but it's still something I practice with my family to this day. Each night the three of us sit at our tiny little kitchen table and share our days. By doing that, we share our lives.

These simple recipes have been developed specifically for easy weeknight preparation so you can get supper on the table quickly and without much hassle.

Easy Smothered Chicken

I'll never forget the first time my mother pulled this amazing smelling concoction out of the oven. The ooey-gooey deliciousness had me at the first bite. It is still a family favorite and continues to receive rave reviews on the blog. One thing that seems to trip folks up is the cream of chicken and mushroom soup. It's just one can that is cream of chicken soup with mushrooms in it. If you can't find it, don't worry. One or the other will work just fine.

1/2 pound bacon

1 1/2 pounds boneless, skinless chicken tenders

Salt and black pepper

1/2 cup all-purpose flour

1 medium onion, sliced

1 (10 3/4-ounce) can cream of chicken and mushroom soup

1 cup water

2 cups shredded Italian blend cheese

Cooked hot white rice

Preheat the oven to 350°. Grease a 13 x 9-inch baking dish.

In a large pan over medium heat, cook the bacon until crispy. Remove it to paper towels to drain and allow it to cool before crumbling.

Season the chicken tenders with salt and pepper, and lightly coat with flour. Lightly brown the chicken in the bacon grease on medium heat for 3 to 4 minutes on each side. Place the chicken in the baking dish and top with the sliced onion.

In a small bowl combine the cream of chicken and mushroom soup with 1 cup of water, and pour over the chicken. Bake uncovered for 25 to 30 minutes, or until the chicken is cooked through.

Remove from the oven; top the chicken with the cheese and crumbled bacon. Return to the oven for 5 to 7 minutes, or until the cheese is melted and bubbly. Serve over hot white rice.

Serves 4 to 6

There's a local seafood buffet restaurant that serves some of the best Shrimp Creole. This recipe is my attempt at recreating it at home. And though it's not exact, it's a pretty close copycat.

In a large Dutch oven heat the oil over medium heat. Add the onion, bell pepper, and celery; cook until the onions are translucent, 7 to 8 minutes. Add the garlic, and cook 30 to 45 seconds, being cautious not to burn it. Stir in the tomatoes with the juice and chicken broth. Bring to a simmer, and add the Creole seasoning and hot sauce. Add the shrimp and cook until they are pink and cooked through. Serve over hot white rice.

Serves 4 to 6

- 3 tablespoons vegetable oil
- 1 yellow onion, chopped
- 1 medium bell pepper, chopped (your choice of color)
- 1 rib celery, chopped
- 3 garlic cloves, minced
- 1 (28-ounce) can diced tomatoes, undrained
- 1 cup chicken broth
- 1 to 2 tablespoons Creole seasoning
- Dash of hot sauce
- 2 to 2 ½ pounds raw shrimp, peeled and deveined
- Cooked hot white rice

This is another one of those recipes from my childhood that makes me long for days past. I always got excited when Mom would announce that it was Porcupine Ball night. These yummy little meatballs get kicked up a notch with the use of tomato-vegetable juice cocktail.

In a large bowl combine the ground beef, rice, onion, and garlic. Mix until just combined, but do not over-work the mixture. Roll the mixture into 1 1/2- to 2-inch balls. In a large nonstick skillet over medium heat, brown the meatballs on several sides and remove from the pan. Drain the grease, and return the pan to the heat. Add the tomato-vegetable juice, tomato paste, salt, and pepper to the pan, and stir to combine. Bring to a simmer, and then add the meatballs back to the pan. Cook 15 to 20 minutes or until the meatballs are cooked through.

Serves 4 to 6

1 1/2 pounds ground beef

3/4 cup instant rice

1/2 small onion, finely diced

1 clove garlic, minced

3 cups tomato-vegetable juice cocktail

1 (6-ounce) can tomato paste

1 teaspoon salt

1/4 teaspoon black pepper

Sour Cream Chicken Enchilada Pie

This recipe is the creation of my amazing, sweet wife, Heather. We've been making sour cream chicken enchiladas for years. One night she came home and said, "Stace, I've got this crazy idea." Normally that phrase would send me running for the hills, but I listened, we put our heads together, and this dish was born. It's been in the regular rotation ever since.

3 cups shredded cooked chicken

1 cup jarred salsa

1 (1-ounce) package taco seasoning

1 (8-ounce) container sour cream

1 (10 3/4-ounce) can cream of chicken soup

1 (4-ounce) can chopped green chilies

1 teaspoon garlic powder

6 to 8 small (about 5.5 inch) corn tortillas

2 cups shredded Mexican cheese blend, divided

Preheat the oven to 350°. Grease a 9-inch deep-dish pie plate.

In a medium bowl combine the cooked chicken, salsa, and taco seasoning. Mix well and set aside.

In another bowl stir together the sour cream, cream of chicken soup, chilies, and garlic powder.

Spread a few tablespoons of the sour cream sauce in the bottom of the pie plate. Top with a layer of tortillas, cutting some in half if necessary to make them cover the bottom of the dish. Top the tortillas with half the chicken mixture, half of the sour cream sauce, and 1 cup of the Mexican cheese blend. Add another layer of tortillas; then repeat the layers with the remaining chicken, sour cream sauce, and remaining cheese.

Bake 20 to 30 minutes or until the cheese is melted and bubbly and the pie is heated through.

Serves 4 to 6

One of the best things about this recipe is that you can tailor it to fit your tastes. If you like mushrooms and green peppers, just add them. If you like it on your pizza, it will taste great in this easy casserole.

1 (12-ounce) package bowtie pasta

1 pound ground beef

1 pound ground sausage

1 small onion, chopped

1 garlic clove, minced

1 (16-ounce) jar pizza sauce

1 (3.5-ounce) package pepperoni

1 (10 3/4-ounce) can condensed Cheddar cheese soup

2 teaspoons salt

2 cups shredded Italian cheese blend

2 cups shredded mozzarella cheese

Preheat the oven to 350°. Grease a 13 x 9-inch baking dish.

Cook the pasta in a large pot per the package directions. Drain the pasta, and return it to the pot.

In a large skillet over medium heat, brown the ground beef, sausage, and onion until the meat is no longer pink. Add the garlic, and cook an additional 2 minutes. Drain the grease, and return the meat mixture to the pan. Stir in the pizza sauce, pepperoni, Cheddar cheese soup, salt, and Italian cheese blend to the meat mixture.

Add the meat mixture to the pot with the cooked pasta, and stir to combine. Pour the mixture into the baking dish. Top with mozzarella cheese. Bake 20 minutes or until the cheese is melted and bubbly.

Serves 5 to 6

If the name alone doesn't sell you, let me give you a rundown: crispy bacon on top of ooey-gooey macaroni and cheese that has been drizzled with cool, tangy ranch dressing. See what I mean? I bet even your picky eaters will go for this.

Preheat the oven to 350°. Grease a 13 x 9-inch baking dish.

Combine the macaroni, chicken, crumbled bacon, cheese soup, cheese, garlic powder, salt, and 1 cup ranch dressing in a very large bowl; mix well.

Turn out into the baking dish. Bake 30 to 35 minutes or until the cheese is melted and the casserole is heated through. Top with the remaining 1/4 cup ranch dressing, and serve immediately.

Serves 5 to 6

One of the best things about recipes like this is that you can get a head start on weeknight preparation by doing things like cooking the bacon and pasta in advance, say, on the weekend. Both items will store well in the refrigerator for a few days until you're ready to use them.

1 (1-pound) package elbow or corkscrew macaroni, cooked per package instructions

4 cups cooked, shredded chicken breast

1 (12-ounce) package bacon, cooked and crumbled

1 (10 3/4-ounce) can condensed Cheddar cheese soup

3 cups shredded Cheddar cheese

1 teaspoon garlic powder

1/2 teaspoon salt

1 1/4 cup prepared ranch dressing, divided

Cheesy Hamburger Skillet

Skip the box mix, and give this a try. It's another one of those dishes that I'm sure even the pickiest of eaters will enjoy. Try swapping out the ground beef for ground turkey or chicken for a different, lighter version. You can even add in some of your favorite vegetables when you add the garlic to make it a complete meal.

1 ½ cups elbow macaroni

1 ½ pounds ground beef

1 small onion, chopped

1 clove garlic, minced

1 (0.87-ounce) package brown gravy mix

1 cup water

1 can condensed Cheddar cheese soup

1 cup shredded Cheddar cheese

Cook the macaroni according to the package directions and drain. In a large skillet over medium heat, brown the ground beef and onions until the beef is cooked through and no longer pink. Drain the excess grease. Return the meat mixture to the hot pan and add the garlic. Cook 1 to 2 minutes or until the garlic is fragrant. Add the brown gravy mix and water. Mix thoroughly. Add the can of Cheddar cheese soup, and stir to combine. Next, add the drained pasta and Cheddar cheese, and stir until the cheese has melted and the mixture is bubbly. Serve alongside a fresh garden salad.

Serves 4 to 6

If you've never had baked spaghetti like this, you should try it. I had a reader ask me if I thought the cream cheese really made a difference. She tried it and replied back to me, "It may not get better than this. The cream cheese gives it a yummy, smooth, velvety texture that is amazing!" I think that's a pretty good recommendation, if you ask me.

Preheat the oven to 350°. Spray a 13 x 9-inch baking dish with nonstick cooking spray.

Cook the spaghetti according to package directions and drain. In a large skillet over medium heat, cook the ground beef and onion until the beef is no longer pink. Drain the excess grease. Return the beef and onion to the pan, and stir in the spaghetti sauce. Bring the meat sauce to a simmer, and cook about 10 minutes.

In another small bowl combine the cream cheese, milk, and garlic powder. In the baking dish layer the noodles, then the cream cheese mixture, then the meat sauce. Top with the mozzarella, and bake 25 to 30 minutes or until the cheese is melted and bubbly.

Serves 5 to 6

- 1 (12-ounce) package thin spaghetti
- 1 1/2 pounds ground beef
- 1 small onion, diced
- 1 (24-ounce) jar spaghetti sauce
- 1 (8-ounce) package cream cheese, softened
- 2 tablespoons milk
- 1/2 teaspoon garlic powder
- 2 cups shredded mozzarella cheese

Sloppy Joes are just one of those things that you either love or hate. My wife had only ever had the stuff out of the can and hated it. That is, until she tasted my homemade version. Now Sloppy Joes make a regular appearance at our house.

In a large skillet over medium heat, brown the beef, onion, and bell pepper until the meat is cooked through and the vegetables are tender. Drain the excess grease, and return the meat mixture to the pan. With the pan over medium-low heat, add the garlic powder, ketchup, brown sugar, mustard, cider vinegar, and soy sauce. Mix well, and simmer for 5 to 10 minutes. Serve on soft hamburger buns.

Serves 5 to 6

1 1/2 pounds ground beef

1 small onion, finely chopped

1 small green bell pepper, seeded and finely chopped

1/4 teaspoon garlic powder

1 cup ketchup

2 tablespoons brown sugar

2 teaspoons prepared mustard

1 tablespoon cider vinegar

1 tablespoon soy sauce

1 package hamburger buns

CHICKEN POT PIE

Everyone knows that Chicken Pot Pie is one of those ultimate comfort foods. But what everyone doesn't know is how easy it can be to put a hearty, delicious pot pie on the table. Use a grocery store rotisserie chicken pieced up, and you'll be sitting down to enjoy this meal in less than an hour.

2 cups shredded cooked chicken

1 (10 3/4-ounce) can cream of chicken soup

1 (15-ounce) can mixed vegetables, drained

1 teaspoon soy sauce

1/8 teaspoon black pepper

1 (14.1-ounce) package refrigerated piecrusts

Preheat the oven to 425°. In a large bowl combine the chicken, cream of chicken soup, mixed vegetables, soy sauce, and pepper. Stir gently to combine. Unroll the piecrusts, and place one in a 9-inch pie plate, being sure to fully cover the sides of the plate. Pour the filling into the piecrust. Top with the other piecrust, and crimp the edges together with a fork or pinch together with your fingers. Cut a few small slits in the center of the top crust to allow the steam to escape. Bake 35 to 40 minutes or until the crust is golden brown and the filling is heated through.

Serves 5 to 6

Stuffed Peppers

Not all quick and easy recipes are suitable for company, but I certainly think this one is worthy. These quick and easy stuffed peppers pack a lot of flavor and look just about as good as they taste.

4 medium-size bell peppers (your choice of color)

1 tablespoon vegetable oil

1 small onion, diced

2 cloves garlic, minced

1 1/2 pounds ground beef

1 (15 1/4-ounce) can seasoned tomato sauce for meatloaf

1 cup instant white rice

1 teaspoon salt

1/8 teaspoon black pepper

1 (8-ounce) can tomato sauce

Preheat the oven to 350°. Bring a large pot of water to a boil over high heat.

Cut the tops off the peppers. Remove the stems; finely dice the pepper tops, and set aside. Scoop out and discard the seeds and membranes. When the water begins boiling, add a large pinch of salt and stir. Add the peppers, and blanch for 5 minutes. Remove them with long-handled tongs or a slotted spoon, and drain them well in a colander or on paper towels.

Grease an 8 x 8-inch baking dish and set aside. Heat the oil in a large skillet over medium heat. Add the onion and the reserved diced bell pepper tops. Cook 7 to 8 minutes or until the onion is translucent. Add the garlic, and cook 30 to 45 seconds or until fragrant. Remove from the heat.

In a large bowl combine the raw ground beef, sautéed onion and pepper mixture, seasoned tomato sauce, white rice, salt, and pepper. Mix until just combined.

Stuff the mixture into each of the peppers and place them upright in the baking dish. Pour the tomato sauce over the peppers. Bake 40 to 50 minutes or until the stuffing is cooked through.

Serves 4

Lasagna Soup

Brandie Skibinski
Salem, Virginia

Brandie whipped up this recipe one night out of desperation. Her husband doesn't like pasta—God love him—but she can get him to eat lasagna. She was all set to turn out a delicious lasagna and realized she had no ricotta or cottage cheese. A box of chicken broth and thirty minutes later, her Lasagna Soup was born.

In a large pot over medium heat, brown the ground beef, onion, and bell pepper until the meat is no longer pink. Add the garlic during the last couple of minutes so it doesn't burn. Drain the excess grease from the beef mixture, and return the beef mixture to the pot. Stir in the thyme, Italian seasoning, salt, brown sugar, chicken broth, diced tomatoes with juice, and tomato sauce. Stir well, and bring the mixture to a boil over medium-high heat. Cover, reduce the heat to a simmer, and cook 20 minutes.

Add the broken lasagna noodles. Simmer about 10 minutes or until the noodles are tender. Stir in the Parmesan cheese.

Ladle the soup into bowls, and sprinkle with mozzarella cheese.

Serves 4 to 6

1 pound ground beef

1 small onion, chopped

1 green bell pepper, chopped

3 cloves garlic, minced

1 teaspoon ground thyme

2 teaspoons Italian seasoning

1/2 teaspoon salt

1 tablespoon firmly packed brown sugar

1 (32-ounce) box chicken broth

2 (14 1/2-ounce) cans petite diced tomatoes

1 (15-ounce) can tomato sauce

2 cups broken lasagna noodles (about 6 whole noodles, broken)

1/2 cup grated Parmesan cheese

2 cups shredded mozzarella cheese

This dish is traditionally something that takes a bit of time to put together. By using quick-cooking, tender pork steaks, we take the prep time from several hours to just shy of one. There's lots of flavor packed in this dish, and it goes great with My Secret Cheese Grits.

cut Pork Tenderloin

2 pounds cubed pork steaks

3 tablespoons vegetable oil

1/3 cup all-purpose flour

1/2 teaspoon salt

1/4 teaspoon black pepper

1/2 teaspoon garlic powder

1 medium onion, chopped

1 medium green bell pepper, seeded and chopped

1 (1.41-ounce) packet roast pork gravy mix

3 cups water

My Secret Cheese Grits (page 47)

Trim and cut the pork steaks into 1-inch strips. Heat the oil in a large skillet over medium-high heat. In a shallow bowl stir together the flour, salt, pepper, and garlic powder. Lightly dredge the pork in the flour mixture, and brown it in the hot oil for 4 to 5 minutes on each side. Remove the pork from the pan, and cover the pork to keep it warm. Add the onion and bell pepper to the skillet, and cook until the onion is translucent.

In a medium bowl combine the gravy mix with the water. Stir well. Pour the gravy mixture into the hot skillet and bring to a boil, stirring frequently. Return the pork to the pan, reduce the heat to low, and simmer, covered, for 35 to 40 minutes. Serve over My Secret Cheese Grits.

Serves 4 to 6

My Secret Cheese Grits

This recipe, as the name implies, offers up the secret to my famous cheese grits. These go great with the Grits and Grillades, or Shrimp and Grits, and they are just wonderful by themselves for breakfast. The cream cheese gives them a smooth, velvety texture that can't be beat.

In a medium saucepan, bring the water to a boil and stir in the salt. Slowly add the grits, stirring constantly to prevent lumps. Reduce the heat to low, cover, and simmer, stirring occasionally, for 15 to 20 minutes or until they reach the desired tenderness and consistency. Grits should be smooth and creamy, not chewy. Add more water if they begin to dry out.

Just before serving, stir in the cream cheese, Cheddar cheese, and butter. Stir until melted and combined. Serve immediately.

Serves 4 to 5

- 5 cups water
- 1 1/2 teaspoons salt
- 1 cup quick-cooking grits
- 3 ounces cream cheese, cut into cubes
- 3/4 cup shredded Cheddar cheese
- 2 tablespoons butter

Lemon-Pepper Catfish

I fondly remember spending the day with my grandfather catching catfish out of a local pond. We'd come home, and he'd cook them outside in a propane fish fryer with his world-famous hush puppies. No fancy gourmet meal could ever beat that one. My version incorporates some lemon-pepper seasoning that I really enjoy with catfish.

CATFISH:

4 to 6 catfish fillets (about 1 1/2 pounds)

Peanut or vegetable oil for frying

3/4 cup cornmeal

1/2 cup all-purpose flour

3 teaspoons garlic powder

3 tablespoons lemon-pepper seasoning

Tartar Sauce (recipe follows)

Rinse catfish fillets under cool water, and lightly pat dry. Pour the oil into a deep cast-iron skillet to a little less than halfway full. Heat the oil over medium-high heat until the oil reaches between 325° and 350°.

In a shallow bowl stir together the cornmeal, flour, garlic powder, and lemon-pepper seasoning. Coat each fillet in the breading mixture, pressing lightly to ensure a thick crust. Fry in batches for 3 to 4 minutes on each side or until golden brown and cooked through. Drain on paper towels. Serve with Tartar Sauce.

Serves 4 to 6

TARTAR SAUCE:

1 cup mayonnaise

1/2 cup dill pickle relish

1 tablespoon grated onion

2 tablespoons fresh lemon juice

In a small bowl mix the mayonnaise, pickle relish, onion, and lemon juice. Refrigerate for at least 30 minutes to allow the flavors to develop.

Serves 6 to 8

Godfather Casserole

SUSAN WILLARD
CONROE, TEXAS

"Godfather night" was always a big event with Susan's son and his friends. It seems extra folks would often show up when word got out what she was making. When her son became a marine and was stationed away, he called in desperation one night longing for this dish. She gave him a grocery list and then walked him through the recipe over the phone. It became an instant hit with his buddies too.

Preheat the oven to 350°. Lightly grease a 13 x 9-inch baking dish. Cook the egg noodles according to the package instructions.

In a large skillet over medium heat, brown the ground beef until it is no longer pink. Drain the excess grease from the meat. Return the meat to the skillet, add the spaghetti sauce, and bring to a simmer.

In a small bowl combine the cream cheese and sour cream.

Place the cooked noodles in the bottom of the baking dish. Layer the cream cheese mixture on top of the noodles, and then pour the meat mixture on top. Bake 25 to 30 minutes or until hot and bubbly.

Remove from the oven, top with the mozzarella cheese, and return to the oven until the cheese has melted.

Serves 6 to 8

1 (16-ounce) package egg noodles

1 pound lean ground beef

1 (24-ounce) jar spaghetti sauce

1 (8-ounce) package cream cheese, softened

1 (8-ounce) container sour cream

2 cups shredded mozzarella cheese

When my wife and I were dating, this was one of her favorite things for my mom to make, but the dish was nameless until she had a dream about it. In her dream she called it Top to Bottom Ham and Cheese Bread, and the name just stuck. And trust me, it might sound simple, but it's good enough to dream about!

Preheat the oven to 350°. Cut the loaves of bread in half lengthwise. Combine the mayonnaise and Cheddar cheese in a small bowl. Spread the mixture on both sides of both loaves of bread. Place the thinly sliced onion and ham in each sandwich to your liking.

Place the sandwiches back together, and wrap them in aluminum foil. Bake 15 to 20 minutes or until the cheese is melted and the sandwiches are heated through.

Serves 6 to 8

- 2 loaves thin crusty French bread
- 1 cup mayonnaise
- 2 cups finely shredded sharp Cheddar cheese
- ~~1/2 medium onion, thinly sliced~~
- 8 to 10 ounces thinly sliced smoked ham

So much of my inspiration for new recipes comes from dishes that I've had at a restaurant somewhere. This is no exception. There's a great local place that serves what they call Corn Soup that I just love. So I set out to recreate it in my kitchen. This is the result, and it sure is good!

4 cups chicken broth

2 (10-ounce) cans tomatoes with green chilies

1 (10 3/4-ounce) can cream of chicken soup

1 1/2 teaspoons garlic powder

1 1/2 teaspoons onion powder

1 teaspoon salt

1 pound process cheese spread, cubed

4 ounces cream cheese, cubed

4 cups cooked, shredded chicken

1 (28-ounce) package frozen whole kernel corn

In a large pot heat the broth over medium-high heat until boiling. Reduce the heat, and add in the tomatoes with the juice, cream of chicken soup, garlic powder, onion powder, and salt. Bring the mixture to a simmer, and then stir in the cubed process cheese spread and cream cheese. Stir until melted, being careful to keep the heat low enough to not scorch the cheese. Once the cheeses have melted, add the cooked chicken and corn. Return the pot to a gentle simmer, and allow the corn to cook through for at least 5 minutes.

Serves 5 to 6

SHRIMP AND GRITS

Shrimp and Grits is about as Southern as screen doors and sweet tea. The flavors of the dish range a bit depending on where you're eating it, but it's all good. This smoky, garlicky version is my favorite. Sometimes I add in 1 cup of sliced mushrooms for a little bit of a different flavor.

4 slices bacon

5 green onions, chopped

3 garlic cloves, minced

16 ounces medium raw, peeled, and deveined shrimp

1/4 teaspoon salt

1/4 teaspoon black pepper

3 tablespoons all-purpose flour

1 cup chicken broth

Dash of hot sauce

Juice of 1 lemon

My Secret Cheese Grits (page 47)

In a large skillet over medium heat, cook the bacon until crispy. Drain the bacon on paper towels; crumble it when it has cooled. Add the chopped onions to the bacon grease in the skillet, and cook over medium heat for 4 to 5 minutes. Add the garlic, and cook until it is fragrant. Sprinkle the shrimp with the salt and pepper, and then add them to the skillet. Cook the shrimp until they are just starting to turn pink, about 3 to 4 minutes.

In a small bowl whisk the flour into the broth. Pour the broth over the shrimp, bring just to a simmer, and cook until the sauce thickens. Stir in the hot sauce and lemon juice, and serve immediately over My Secret Cheese Grits (page 47).

Serves 4 to 5

When I tell folks that my childhood tastes like Goulash, some laugh at me, but I'm very serious. This comforting, hearty dish takes me back to a time when I could barely see above the top of the kitchen table. I can almost feel my legs dangling beneath the chair. I love how food can remind us of our past like that.

In a large Dutch oven brown the ground beef over medium-high heat until it is no longer pink. Drain the grease. Add the onion and garlic to the meat, and reduce the heat to medium. Cook until the onion is translucent. Add the tomato sauce, diced tomatoes with juice, water, paprika, salt, and pepper. Reduce the heat, and simmer uncovered for 15 to 20 minutes, stirring occasionally. Stir in the corn and uncooked macaroni, and simmer uncovered for 20 minutes or until the macaroni is tender. Serve sprinkled with shredded Cheddar cheese.

Serves 6 to 8

1 1/2 pounds ground beef

1 large onion, diced

3 cloves garlic, minced

1 (28-ounce) can tomato sauce

1 (28-ounce) can diced tomatoes

3 cups water

1 tablespoon paprika

2 teaspoons salt

1 teaspoon black pepper

1 (15 1/4-ounce) can whole kernel corn, drained

2 cups uncooked elbow macaroni

Shredded Cheddar cheese

WISDOM FROM THE PEANUT MAN

A FEW YEARS AGO I WAS IN A DOWNTOWN AREA WHEN A MAN approached me begging for money. He told me that his wife was pregnant and that he was stranded. He said he needed money to put some gas in his car to get back to her. Having recently had a pregnant wife, I felt sorry for him and I reached down into my pockets and gave him all the cash I had. I then went about my day feeling like I had done something good.

Two weeks later I had business back downtown and found myself in the same area as the previous encounter. I was startled when the same man came up to me and offered the same story begging for money. To say the least, I was rattled. I had been duped.

After that, it was hard for me to trust people who were begging for money, but all that changed one Friday. I had run by a fast-food joint for a quick lunch and was on my way out of the drive-through when I noticed a man in a wheelchair by the exit. He was holding a ragged cardboard box and a small sign. I stopped and rolled down my window. He asked me if I'd like to buy some peanuts. He said he was selling roasted and boiled. And while I love both kinds, I knew I had several pounds of peanuts at home leftover from a birthday party.

At first I was tempted to offer him my usual "no, thanks" and drive away, but something was different about this guy. In addition to being wheelchair bound, he was wearing tattered clothes and had an expression that I will never be able to erase from my memory. He was tired. Not just from doing his best to maneuver his wheelchair around what was a scorching hot parking lot, but tired from life. He had the look of someone who had spent his entire life trying, but never succeeding. The wrinkles on his face were evidence of time—a time that had not been kind to him. I grabbed a $5 bill—it was all I had, I never carry cash with me—and handed it to him through the window. He tried his best to get me to take some peanuts, but I refused. I told him he could take those and sell them to someone else. He insisted again, but I told him no . . . that I didn't even like peanuts. He looked me in the eyes and told me thank you, and as I turned back to pull away, he called to me and said, "God bless you, sir."

Those simple words penetrated me like few words ever have—all the way to my soul. I realized at that very second that it isn't my job to judge why someone is begging for money or question their plan for it. It was heavy on my heart that day to give him what I had. So I did. The truth is, he could have wheeled his rear down the street and gotten in a brand-new car. I'll never know. But what I do know is that doing that made me feel good. He wasn't out there just begging; he was trying his best to sell those peanuts and do what he could to make a living for himself. I respect that. And he made me realize that people like him are put in my path for a reason. They aren't there to be judged or second-guessed.

While it certainly does my heart good to be able to help someone like him, it's not really about that either. Sometimes people like him are put into our paths to make us realize how fortunate we each are. While that $5 might have helped to feed his family that night, that $5 fed my soul. You can't put a price on that. We get so caught up in life that we fuss and complain when we see a sink piled high with dirty dishes, but we should be thankful because those dirty dishes mean we were able to feed our families. There are so many out there who would give everything to have a sink piled high with dirty dinner dishes. Think about that . . .

WEEKEND BITES

THE WEEKEND OFTEN AFFORDS US A LITTLE MORE TIME TO ENJOY being in the kitchen preparing a meal for our families. Having a full-time job that isn't blogging, I find that my weekends are often spent cooking and developing recipes for the blog. I also use the weekend to make special desserts or meals that we can have as leftovers through-out the next week.

Sunday supper has always been a big deal in the South. It was traditionally the largest meal of the week. For poor Southerners who were farmers and sharecroppers, most meals consisted of whatever vegetables and starches they had on hand, but Sunday's meal was the one that often boasted meat. Often that meat was some form of cured pork, be it smoked or salt cured. Back then, people threw noth-ing away, so the leftover pork bones were used to season vegetables throughout the next week. This tradition carries over to today not only because of practicality but also because that is the way many of us were raised. The food of our parents and grandparents was the food of the poor agrarian society. Folks made do with what they had.

Cooking the food of the people before us keeps us connected to them.

The recipes in this chapter might take a little more time and attention, but I've included some great easy ideas for weeknight meals that take advantage of some of the leftovers.

59

Every Southern cook dreams of perfecting a fried chicken recipe. I've been working on it for years. This recipe requires an overnight soaking in a buttermilk marinade, but trust me; it's worth every single second.

3 cups buttermilk

3 tablespoons salt

2 tablespoons sugar

1 tablespoon black pepper

2 teaspoons garlic powder

1 1/2 teaspoons hot sauce

2 to 3 pounds bone-in chicken pieces

Peanut oil or vegetable oil for frying

2 cups all-purpose flour

In a large glass or plastic bowl, combine the buttermilk, salt, sugar, pepper, garlic powder, and hot sauce. Add the chicken to the buttermilk marinade, cover, and refrigerate for 12 to 24 hours.

When ready to fry, heat about 1 inch of oil in the bottom of a deep Dutch oven over medium-high heat. Place the flour in a large shallow dish or pie plate. Drain the marinade from the chicken, and dredge the chicken in the flour, then shake off the excess. Once the oil has reached 350°, fry the chicken in batches for 10 to 12 minutes on each side, or until the chicken is golden brown and cooked through. You may need to adjust the heat so that the oil stays around 325°; a deep-fry thermometer is very handy for this. Drain on paper towels.

Serves 6 to 8

This stuff is good on just about everything. It's great slathered on fried chicken, French fries, or anything fried, for that matter. And just like the name implies, it will keep folks coming back for more. We just about always keep some of this in a jar in the refrigerator.

In a small bowl combine the mayonnaise, chili sauce, garlic powder, pepper, and onion powder, and refrigerate for several hours to allow the flavors to develop.

Serves 5 to 6

- 3/4 cup mayonnaise
- 1/3 cup chili sauce
- 1/2 teaspoon garlic powder
- 1/2 teaspoon black pepper
- 1/4 teaspoon onion powder

Chicken Bog

I grew up eating Chicken Bog. My mother lived in South Carolina for a while, and that's where she picked up the dish. Many folks have never even heard of it. I liken it to a kicked-up version of chicken and rice. Some folks also call this dish Chicken Pilau.

1 (3- to 4-pound) whole chicken, cut up

1 pound smoked sausage, sliced

1/2 cup (1 stick) butter

1 tablespoon soy sauce

2 cups uncooked rice

Salt and black pepper

Place the chicken pieces in the bowl of a 4-quart slow cooker and cover with water. Cover and cook on low for 8 to 10 hours. Once cooked, remove from the slow cooker and cool slightly. Pick the meat from the chicken and discard the skin and bones.

Discard the fat and chicken pieces in the broth by carefully pouring the chicken broth from the slow cooker through a strainer into a large stock pot. Place the stock pot over medium-high heat, and bring the broth to a boil. Add the sliced sausage, butter, soy sauce, and rice. Stir well. Reduce the heat to a simmer, and cook until the rice is almost done, usually 15 to 20 minutes, adding additional water if necessary. Return the chicken to the pot, stir to combine, and finish cooking the rice. Add salt and pepper to taste.

Serves 6 to 8

Meatloaf is one of those things that everybody has a recipe for. In terms of mine, I like to cook the meatloaf in the center of a 13 x 9-inch baking dish to allow some of the fat to drain away. It seems to hold up better that way too. Of course, the best thing about meatloaf is the leftover meatloaf sandwich the next day.

Preheat the oven to 350°. In a small bowl stir the bread crumbs and milk together. Set aside to allow the bread crumbs to absorb the milk completely. In a large bowl combine the soaked bread crumbs, ground beef, onion, bell pepper, egg, soy sauce, garlic powder, salt, and black pepper. Mix well with your hands.

Form into a loaf in the middle of a 13 x 9-inch baking dish. In a small bowl mix together the ketchup, mustard, and brown sugar. Spread over the top of the meatloaf. Bake uncovered for 1 hour to 1 hour and 10 minutes or until the meatloaf is cooked through.

Serves about 6

1/2 cup plain bread crumbs

1/2 cup milk

1 1/2 pounds lean ground beef

1/2 small onion, finely diced

1/2 small green bell pepper, finely diced

1 large egg, slightly beaten

1 tablespoon soy sauce

1/2 teaspoon garlic powder

1 teaspoon salt

1/4 teaspoon black pepper

1/3 cup ketchup

1 1/2 tablespoons prepared mustard

1 tablespoon brown sugar

Mississippi Roast

Vicki Kleppelid
Ridgeland, Mississippi

When Vicki's sister-in-law made this recipe for her, she knew she had to share it with me. When I made this recipe and tasted it, I knew I had to share it with y'all. It is so easy, but it is packed with amazing flavor. I even strained the broth in the crockpot and reduced it down on the stovetop in a saucepan to make a delicious gravy.

1 (4- to 5-pound) chuck or sirloin tip roast

1 (1-ounce) package ranch salad dressing mix

1 (0.6- to 1.0-ounce) package au jus mix

½ cup (1 stick) butter

5 pepperoncini peppers

Place the roast in the bowl of a 4-quart slow cooker. Sprinkle the roast with the ranch dressing and au jus mixes. Place the stick of butter on top of the roast with the peppers. Cover and cook on low for 7 to 8 hours. Serve alongside creamy mashed potatoes and your favorite vegetable.

Serves 4 to 6

Top Round low 5 hrs.

WEEKNIGHT LEFTOVERS: POT ROAST PO-BOY SANDWICH

Shred the leftover beef, and reheat it in a saucepan with the cooking liquid from the crockpot. Serve the roast on crusty French bread for an authentic-tasting "Debris" Po-Boy sandwich.

My favorite way to eat pork chops is right off the smoking hot grill, but this recipe is a close second. You can easily change up this recipe by swapping out the cream of onion soup for your favorite. I'm sure cream of mushroom would be just as good.

In a large skillet heat the oil over medium-high heat. Season the pork chops with salt and pepper. Brown the pork chops in hot oil for 3 to 4 minutes on each side. Remove the chops to a plate, and set aside. Slowly add the water to the hot pan and stir well. Add the onion soup, and mix well. Bring the mixture to a simmer. Return the pork chops to the pan, and top with the sliced onions. Simmer for 55 to 60 minutes or until the pork chops are tender.

Serves 4 to 5

2 tablespoons vegetable oil

2 to 3 pounds pork chops

2 teaspoons salt

1/4 teaspoon black pepper

1 cup water

1 (10 3/4-ounce) can cream of onion condensed soup

1 onion, thinly sliced

STUFFED CABBAGE

My mom always made this in a big electric skillet. Anytime I saw that skillet come out, I knew it was Stuffed Cabbage night. It has always been one of my most favorite recipes that she makes and has been my dish of choice to celebrate many special occasions.

7 to 8 large cabbage leaves

2 1/2 pounds lean ground beef

1 small onion, finely chopped

1 teaspoon salt

1/4 teaspoon black pepper

1/2 teaspoon garlic powder

1 large egg, beaten

1 (46-ounce) bottle tomato-vegetable juice cocktail

a little sugar

In a large pot of salted boiling water, blanch the cabbage leaves for 8 to 10 minutes or until they are soft and pliable, but not soft enough to easily tear. Remove and set aside.

Meanwhile, combine the ground beef, onion, salt, pepper, garlic powder, and egg. Mix until just combined. Scoop out about 3/4 to 1 cup of the mixture, and roll it into a large oval-shaped ball. Place the meatball at the base of a blanched cabbage leaf near the stem and roll up, tucking the edges in as you go. Repeat until you've used all of the filling.

Place the stuffed cabbage rolls in a large pan or Dutch oven with a lid, and add the tomato-vegetable juice until it just covers the cabbage. Simmer, covered, for 45 minutes to 1 hour or until the cabbage is tender and the meat is cooked through.

Serves 6 to 8

My mother is the greatest cook I know, so one of the most rewarding things for me is for her to enjoy something I've cooked. This is a new recipe that I developed just for this book. The night my parents joined us for dinner and I served this chicken, my mom took home the leftovers. That just tickled me pink.

Preheat the oven to 400°. In a small bowl mix together the softened butter, salt, pepper, and garlic powder. Rinse the chicken well; then pat it dry with paper towels. Place the chicken in the bottom of a large roasting pan. Rub the butter mixture over the entire chicken, inside the cavity, and between the skin and the breasts. Slice the heads of garlic in half crosswise, and place them inside the cavity.

Tuck the wing tips under the chicken and tie the legs together with cotton kitchen twine. Add the onion, potatoes, and carrots to the bottom of the pan around the chicken. Bake 1 to 1 1/2 hours or until the juices run clear when an inner thigh is pierced. Allow the chicken to rest for 15 minutes before slicing and serving.

Serves 4 to 5

1/2 cup (1 stick) unsalted butter, softened

2 teaspoons salt

1/2 teaspoon black pepper

2 teaspoons garlic powder

1 (5-pound) roasting chicken

2 heads garlic

1 large onion, peeled and sliced

3 large potatoes, cut into 1-inch cubes

4 to 6 carrots, peeled and sliced

WEEKNIGHT LEFTOVER: CHICKEN POT PIE

Use the leftover chicken from this recipe to whip up a simple Chicken Pot Pie (page 42).

Beef Vegetable Soup

As a kid, I would anxiously await fall and the first nip of cold in the air because I knew Mom's vegetable soup would soon follow. She would serve this alongside a grilled cheese sandwich or even a peanut butter and jelly sandwich. I'm in my thirties now, and I still await the phone call that she's making soup.

1 ½ pounds lean beef stew meat

1 large red onion, chopped

7 cups water

1 tablespoon salt

½ teaspoon black pepper

2 pounds lean ground beef

5 to 6 potatoes, chopped

1 (8-ounce) package baby carrots

2 ribs celery, chopped

1 (16-ounce) bag frozen baby lima beans

1 (16-ounce) bag frozen field peas with snaps

1 (16-ounce) bag frozen cut green beans

1 (16-ounce) bag frozen whole kernel corn

1 (28-ounce) can petite diced tomatoes

1 (15-ounce) can tomato sauce

1 tablespoon sugar

1 cup uncooked elbow macaroni

Combine the stew meat, chopped onion, water, salt, and pepper in the bowl of a 4-quart slow cooker. Cover and cook on low for 8 to 10 hours or overnight.

In a large skillet over medium heat, cook the ground beef until no longer pink, and then drain the grease.

Transfer the stew meat and broth from the slow cooker into a large stock pot. Add the drained, cooked ground beef. Add the potatoes, carrots, celery, lima beans, peas, green beans, corn, tomatoes with the juice, and tomato sauce. Cook over medium heat about 30 minutes or until the potatoes are tender.

Stir in the sugar and uncooked elbow macaroni, and add salt and pepper to taste. You might also need to add a bit more water here if you like. Cook about 20 minutes more or until the noodles are cooked to your liking.

Serves 10 to 12

Whether you like your barbecue sweet and sticky or with more of a tangy vinegar flavor, this easy slow-cooker recipe sure beats pulling out the smoker. Just add your favorite barbecue sauce at the end, and you've got a delicious meal.

Add the chopped onion and garlic to the bottom of the bowl of a 4-quart slow cooker. Season the pork butt with the seasoned salt and add it to the bowl. Pour in the cider vinegar, chicken broth, and a few dashes of liquid smoke flavoring. Cover and cook on low for 8 to 10 hours.

After cooking, remove the meat from the slow cooker and shred, discarding the fat. Mix in your favorite barbecue sauce and serve.

Serves 6 to 8

1 large onion, chopped

3 cloves garlic, smashed

1 (5-pound) pork Boston butt

1 tablespoon seasoned salt

1 cup cider vinegar

1/2 cup chicken broth

~~Dash of liquid smoke flavoring~~

Barbecue sauce

WEEKNIGHT LEFTOVERS: BBQ PIZZA

Top a premade pizza dough with barbecue sauce, the leftover pulled pork, sliced onion, and Cheddar cheese for an easy weeknight meal that everyone will love.

The argument over whether jambalaya should have tomatoes or not is just about as fierce as the argument of Creole versus Cajun. I prefer my jambalaya with tomatoes, like this recipe and the Reader Recipe on page 44. But either way, it's good stuff.

1/4 cup vegetable oil

1 large onion, chopped

1 large bell pepper, seeded and chopped (your choice of color)

3 cloves garlic, minced

Crushed red pepper flakes

1 pound Cajun or Andouille smoked sausage, sliced into 3/4-inch rounds

1 pound chicken breast meat, cubed

1 (28-ounce) can diced tomatoes

1 (15-ounce) can tomato sauce

2 bay leaves

1 cup chicken broth

1 teaspoon Creole seasoning

1 1/2 cups uncooked rice

In a large Dutch oven heat the oil over medium heat. Add the onion and bell pepper, and cook until the onion is translucent. Add the garlic and a pinch (or more) of red pepper flakes, and cook until the garlic is fragrant. Add the sausage and chicken, and cook until the chicken is mostly white. Add the tomatoes with the juice, tomato sauce, bay leaves, broth, Creole seasoning, and uncooked rice. Cover, and reduce the heat to a simmer. Cook 45 to 55 minutes, stirring occasionally, or until the rice is tender and most of the liquid has been absorbed. Remove the bay leaves before serving.

Serves 5 to 6

SWEET AND SAVORY GLAZED HAM

One of the best parts of a ham is usually the leftovers. Whether it's the bone in some beans or a soup or fried ham for breakfast, we Southerners can put a hurtin' on some leftover ham. The sweet and tangy glaze works so well with the smoky ham in this recipe though, I bet there won't be many leftovers.

Preheat the oven to 325°. Add about 1/2 cup of water into the bottom of a small roasting pan or baking dish. Add the ham, and cover tightly with aluminum foil. Bake 50 minutes.

In a small bowl prepare the glaze by mixing together the pineapple juice, cider vinegar, ginger, mustard, and garlic powder.

Remove the ham from the oven after 50 minutes and carefully uncover. Baste the ham with the glaze. Return the ham to the oven, and bake uncovered for 20 minutes more.

Serves 10 to 12

1 (5- to 6-pound) fully cooked, smoked ham

1 (6-ounce) can pineapple juice

2 tablespoons cider vinegar

1/2 teaspoon ground ginger

1/4 cup Dijon mustard

1 teaspoon garlic powder

WEEKNIGHT LEFTOVERS: HAM AND SWISS STUFFED BAKED POTATOES

Top hot baked potatoes with leftover chopped ham, Swiss cheese, and some chopped green onions for an easy weeknight meal.

Everyone has a different recipe for this hearty stew, sometimes called Camp Stew. My version is a combination of a recipe from a famed lunchroom lady from Luverne, Alabama, and another family recipe that is generations old. The type of meat varies by recipe. Some include chicken, pork, beef, and even wild game.

1 (5- to 6-pound) broiler-fryer chicken

1 tablespoon salt

1 tablespoon black pepper

2 large onions, chopped

1/4 cup Worcestershire sauce

2/3 cup white vinegar

Juice of 1 lemon (about 3 tablespoons)

1 cup ketchup

1 (28-ounce) can crushed tomatoes

1 (14.5-ounce) can petite diced tomatoes

3 large potatoes, peeled and diced

1 (15 1/4-ounce) can whole kernel corn, drained

1 (14 3/4-ounce) can creamed corn

Hot sauce

Place the chicken in a large stock pot, and just barely cover it with water. Add the salt, pepper, and chopped onion. Bring to a simmer over medium heat, and then cook 40 to 50 minutes, or until the chicken is cooked through. Remove the chicken from the stock. Allow it to cool slightly, and then debone the chicken and shred the meat. Carefully strain any chicken fat from the top of the broth. Return the shredded chicken to the broth. Add the Worcestershire sauce, vinegar, lemon juice, ketchup, crushed tomatoes, and diced tomatoes to the cooking water. Stir to combine. Add the potatoes, and cook 30 minutes over low heat or until the potatoes are just tender. Add the drained whole kernel corn and creamed corn. Cook over very low heat for an additional 15 to 20 minutes, being cautious not to scorch the corn. Add hot sauce to taste.

Serves 10 to 12

Sausage and Cheese Pie

DRU LOVETT
WINFIELD, ALABAMA

For Dru, this is one of those recipes that has been passed around, altered, and updated. This family favorite is kid-friendly as well. I think it would be great for breakfast—or any meal, for that matter.

Preheat the oven to 350° and lightly spray a 9-inch deep-dish pie plate or an 8 x 8-inch baking dish with nonstick cooking spray. Arrange one can of crescent rolls on the bottom and up the sides of the dish to form a crust. Pinch the seams together.

Crumble the sausage into a large skillet over medium heat, and cook until it is no longer pink and is cooked through. Drain the sausage, blotting it with paper towels to remove as much grease as possible. Return the sausage to the skillet, and add the cream cheese, garlic powder, and onion powder. Cook over medium heat, stirring constantly, until the cream cheese has melted. Pour the mixture on top of the first layer of crescents, and spread to cover. Sprinkle the Cheddar cheese on top. Top the mixture with the remaining crescents to form a top crust. Bake 15 to 20 minutes or until the pie is golden brown. Remove from the oven, and allow the pie to cool for 10 minutes before slicing and serving.

Serves 6 to 8

2 (8-ounce) packages crescent rolls (8-count)

1 pound ground pork sausage

1 (8-ounce) package cream cheese, softened

1 teaspoon garlic powder

1 teaspoon onion powder

2 cups shredded sharp Cheddar cheese

SIDE BITES

IN THE SOUTH, SIDE DISHES ARE A BIG DEAL. JUST AS MUCH PREPARA-tion goes into them as the main course. It's not uncommon to see five or six sides on the table at large family gatherings. The abundance of what we call "sides" says a lot about our heritage too. When my grandparents were young, there weren't many meals they had that had meat on the menu. It was expensive, and the meat they did have was usually from whatever chickens or pigs they had on the farm. There wasn't any running down to the supermarket. My grandfather was one of thirteen children. Many of their meals were composed solely of the vegetables and potatoes they grew in their garden. A pot of beans or field peas and a slice of cornbread was often the entire evening meal.

I think that in itself speaks to the kind of people you find in the South. Never have I heard my grandfather complain about having such a meager supper. He and his family were just grateful to have what they had. While we remain a gracious and grateful people, I can't help but wonder what the world would be like if we all could appreciate things the way they did.

One of my readers, Julie Taylor, sent me a great recipe for Okra Fritters several years ago, and they were an instant hit on the blog. This recipe is an adaptation of that original recipe that includes a little cornmeal. If you like fried okra, chances are you'll love these.

1/2 cup all-purpose flour

1/2 cup self-rising cornmeal

1/2 teaspoon salt

1/2 teaspoon black pepper

1 teaspoon garlic powder

1 pound okra, coarsely chopped

1/2 onion, finely diced

1 large egg

1/2 cup buttermilk

1/3 cup vegetable oil

In a large bowl combine the flour, cornmeal, salt, pepper, and garlic powder. Add the chopped okra and onion. In a small bowl lightly beat the egg into the buttermilk, and then add it to the okra mixture. Stir until just combined.

Heat the oil in a large skillet over medium heat. Drop the okra batter into the oil by heaping tablespoonsful. Cook 4 to 5 minutes, then flip the fritters and press them flat with the back of a spatula. Cook 4 to 5 more minutes or until crispy and golden brown. Cook in batches, adding more oil if necessary; then drain on paper towels, and serve hot.

Makes about 12 fritters

The inspiration for this recipe came from a dish I had at a restaurant in Orange Beach, Alabama. After I created it, I couldn't come up with a suitable name. We held a contest on the blog to name it, and the winner was Gumbo Greens. If you like collard greens, these will be a special treat for you.

Combine the water, bouillon cubes, ham hock, salt, garlic, and vinegar in a large stock pot, and bring to a boil over medium-high heat. Add the collards, reduce the heat to medium, and cook 1 hour to 1 1/2 hours to reach the desired tenderness.

Remove the ham hock, and pick and shred the meat. Return the meat to the pot, and discard the bone. Add the okra and tomatoes, and cook 35 to 40 minutes or until the okra just begins to fall apart.

Serves 6 to 8

3 quarts water

3 chicken bouillon cubes

1 smoked ham hock

1 1/2 tablespoons salt

3 garlic cloves, peeled and smashed

2 tablespoons white vinegar

1 bunch collard greens, washed and chopped

1/2 pound okra, chopped

2 tomatoes, seeded and chopped

CORNBREAD SALAD

This recipe is one of the most popular recipes on the entire blog. It's pretty versatile too. Feel free to mix things up by swapping out the pinto beans for black beans or by adding some chopped crispy bacon. Show up to the next potluck with this, and you'll be the hit of the party.

1 (1-ounce) package buttermilk ranch salad dressing mix

1 cup mayonnaise

1/2 cup buttermilk

3 cups coarsely chopped cornbread

1 (14 1/2-ounce) can pinto beans, drained and rinsed

1 (16-ounce) can whole kernel corn, drained

1 small green bell pepper, seeded and finely chopped

1 small sweet onion, finely chopped

2 ripe tomatoes, seeded and chopped

2 cups finely shredded sharp Cheddar cheese

In a small bowl combine the ranch dressing mix, mayonnaise, and buttermilk. Mix well and then refrigerate while you assemble the salad. Layer the salad starting with the chopped cornbread in the bottom of a large trifle or punch bowl. Top the cornbread layer with the rinsed pinto beans. Next, add the drained corn, then the bell pepper, sweet onion, tomatoes, and Cheddar cheese. Pour the ranch dressing mixture on top. Refrigerate for several hours to allow the flavors to develop.

Serves 6 to 8

When we met, my wife was one of the pickiest eaters I knew. I doubted our relationship for a while based on that because I'll eat just about anything. I decided to stick it out: she was worth it. What I found was that when she tasted my versions of things, she liked them more than she wanted to. Today she's a far stretch from the picky eater she once was. For example, she hated cabbage until she tasted this Asian Slaw. Now it's one of her favorite dishes.

Melt the butter in a large skillet over medium heat. Add the crushed ramen noodles (reserving the seasoning packet) and almonds, and cook, stirring frequently, until the ramen noodles are lightly toasted. Remove from the heat, and carefully add the sugar, vinegar, oil, soy sauce, and ramen seasoning packet. Stir to combine, and allow to cool completely.

Empty the coleslaw mix into a large bowl, and add the chopped green onions. Once the ramen mixture is cool, toss with coleslaw mix and serve immediately.

Serves 4 to 5

- 1/4 cup (1/2 stick) butter
- 1 (3-ounce) package chicken-flavor ramen noodles, crushed
- 1/2 cup sliced almonds
- 1/3 cup sugar
- 1/3 cup white vinegar
- 1/3 cup vegetable oil
- 2 tablespoons soy sauce
- 1 (14- to 16-ounce) package bagged classic coleslaw mix
- 5 green onions, chopped

Broccoli Cornbread

EMILY WILLINGHAM
COLUMBIA, SOUTH CAROLINA

Emily says, "This is the best cornbread in the world! It's so moist and flavorful. The cottage cheese makes the recipe, and doesn't overpower it. Cottage cheese haters won't even notice it's in the recipe."

2 (8 ½-ounce) boxes
"JIFFY"® Corn Muffin Mix

4 large eggs, beaten

3/4 cup (1 ½ sticks) butter,
melted

1 (10-ounce) package frozen
chopped broccoli, thawed
and drained

1 medium onion, chopped

1 cup cottage cheese

Preheat the oven to 375°. Combine the corn muffin mix, eggs, butter, broccoli, onion, and cottage cheese in a large bowl. Pour the batter into a lightly greased 13 x 9-inch baking dish. Cook 35 to 40 minutes or until lightly browned.

Serves 8 to 10

STEWED SQUASH AND TOMATOES

I'm not sure if it's the bright colors or the fresh flavors, but this dish just says summer to me. It is always one of the first dishes I make when the roadside fruit and vegetable stands start popping up. You can replace the canned tomatoes with about four seeded and chopped fresh tomatoes.

Cut the squash and zucchini in half lengthwise and slice into 1/4-inch slices. Heat the oil in a large Dutch oven over medium heat. Add the onion, and cook until it becomes translucent. Add the minced garlic, and cook 1 minute. Add the squash, zucchini, and canned tomatoes with the juice. Add salt and pepper to taste. Reduce the heat to a simmer, and cook the mixture 10 to 15 minutes, or until the squash reaches the desired tenderness. Add the chopped basil, and serve.

Serves 5 to 6

- 1/2 pound (about 3) yellow summer squash
- 1/2 pound (about 3) zucchini
- 2 tablespoons vegetable oil
- 1 medium onion, chopped
- 4 garlic cloves, minced
- 1 (28-ounce) can diced tomatoes
- Salt and black pepper
- 4 tablespoons chopped fresh basil

SWEET AND SOUR GREEN BEANS

The sweet and tangy sauce that clings to these green beans brings a little something different to an otherwise normal vegetable. With the smoky flavor from the bacon, I bet even green bean haters will eat these.

In a large skillet over medium heat, cook the bacon until crispy. Remove the bacon from the pan, drain on paper towels, and coarsely chop once it is cooled. Add the green beans to the bacon grease, and cook over medium heat until the beans reach your desired tenderness. In a small bowl whisk together the vinegar, cornstarch, brown sugar, dry mustard, salt, and pepper. Pour the mixture over the green beans, add the chopped bacon back to the pan, and cook until the sauce thickens and coats the beans.

Serves 4 to 6

5 slices bacon

1 (16-ounce) package fresh or frozen green beans (thawed)

1/3 cup white vinegar

2 teaspoons cornstarch

1 tablespoon light brown sugar

1/4 teaspoon dry mustard

1/2 teaspoon salt

1/2 teaspoon black pepper

Hot Tomato and Bacon Pasta

If you're looking for something a little different to serve alongside your meal, try this easy Hot Tomato and Bacon Pasta. You can even add some sliced grilled chicken and turn this delicious side into a spectacular entree.

1 (16-ounce) package bowtie pasta

5 slices bacon

1 large onion, chopped

3 garlic cloves, minced

1 (14.5-ounce) can diced tomatoes

Salt

Cook the pasta according to the package instructions, and drain well.

In a large skillet over medium heat, fry the bacon until crispy; then drain on paper towels and crumble. Drain all but about 3 tablespoons of the bacon grease from the pan. Return the pan to medium heat, add the onion, and cook 7 to 8 minutes or until the onion is just translucent. Add the garlic and the tomatoes with juice. Add salt to taste; then reduce the heat to low, and simmer for 20 minutes. Add the crumbled bacon to the sauce, and then toss with the pasta.

Serves 5 to 6

FRIED OKRA

Fried Okra means different things to different people. In my family, we have two kinds. One is where each round of okra is individually battered and deep fried. The other, like this recipe, is more of a hash. This is the version my grandmother makes, and while I like them both, this is my favorite.

1 pound okra

1 teaspoon salt

1/2 teaspoon black pepper

3/4 cup cornmeal

1/3 cup vegetable oil

Wash the okra, and cut it into about half-inch pieces, discarding the tip and stem ends. Rinse the cut okra under cool water, and drain. Place the okra in a large bowl, and add salt, pepper, and cornmeal to the damp okra. Toss lightly to coat.

Heat the vegetable oil in a cast-iron skillet over medium heat. Carefully add the okra to the pan. Cook about 20 minutes, stirring frequently, or until the okra is browned and cooked through.

Serves 4 to 5

Corn Pudding

BONNIE MCCAWLEY
FAYETTEVILLE, ARKANSAS

This dish was always a part of Bonnie's family's holiday spread in the Northeast. She made this for a holiday gathering after she moved to Arkansas and has been asked to bring it every year since then. You know what that means? It's got to be good!

Preheat the oven to 350°. Grease an 8 x 8-inch baking dish.

Place 1 cup of the corn, eggs, whipping cream, milk, sugar, butter, flour, baking powder, and salt into a blender, and blend until almost smooth. Pour the mixture into the baking dish and top with the remaining 1 cup of corn. Bake 35 to 45 minutes or until the pudding is set in the middle.

Serves 6 to 8

2 cups whole kernel corn, divided

4 large eggs

1 cup whipping cream

1/2 cup milk

6 tablespoons sugar

1/4 cup (1/2 stick) butter, softened

2 tablespoons all-purpose flour

2 teaspoons baking powder

1 teaspoon salt

Apparently quite a bit has been said about the difference between butterbeans and lima beans. In my house, butter beans are the small, mildly flavored beans that are usually light green or speckled. Lima beans have a bolder flavor and are usually darker green. Regardless, this recipe works well with both.

In a large Dutch oven over medium heat, cook the bacon until just barely crispy. Drain away all but about 2 tablespoons of the bacon grease, then return the pan to the heat. Add the chopped onion, and cook until it is translucent, about 7 to 8 minutes. Add the beans, broth, salt, and pepper. Bring the broth to a boil, and then reduce the heat to a simmer and cook about 30 minutes.

Serves 6 to 8

- 6 slices bacon, coarsely chopped
- 1 small onion, chopped
- 1 (28-ounce) bag frozen butter beans (about 5 cups)
- 4 cups chicken broth
- 1 teaspoon salt
- 1/2 teaspoon black pepper

BUTTERMILK MASHED POTATOES

The buttermilk in these mashed potatoes gives the dish a little bit of a tang that you don't find in regular mashed potatoes. If you're not adventurous enough to go that route, just replace the buttermilk with regular milk. This is just a good basic recipe that works either way.

2 pounds baking potatoes

1 teaspoon salt, plus more for seasoning

3 tablespoons butter, melted

3/4 cup buttermilk

Black pepper

Wash, peel, and cut the potatoes into 1-inch cubes. Place the potatoes in a medium-size pot, and add water until the potatoes are covered by about an inch of water. Add the salt, and bring the pot to a boil over medium-high heat. Cook the potatoes 15 to 20 minutes or until they are soft when poked with a fork.

When the potatoes are done, drain them well and return them to the pot. Add the butter and buttermilk. Mash with a potato masher for lumpy potatoes or mix with a hand mixer for a smoother texture. Add salt and pepper to taste.

Serves 4 to 5

COMPANY POTATOES

I named this dish Company Potatoes because having to grate the potatoes takes a little extra work. I usually make them only when company's coming over. It's not that my family doesn't deserve the extra work and all; it's just that they would be happy with instant mashed potatoes. Bless their hearts.

2 pounds baking potatoes

1 cup shredded Cheddar cheese

1 (10 3/4-ounce) can cream of mushroom soup

1 teaspoon garlic powder

1/2 cup sour cream

1/4 cup mayonnaise

1/2 teaspoon black pepper

1 (1-ounce) package ranch salad dressing mix

2 tablespoons plain bread crumbs

3 tablespoons butter, melted

Preheat the oven to 350°. Grease a 13 x 9-inch baking dish.

Wash, peel, and grate the potatoes on the large side of a box grater. Place the potatoes in a colander for a few minutes to allow some of the excess water to drain away.

In a large bowl combine the potatoes, cheese, mushroom soup, garlic powder, sour cream, mayonnaise, pepper, and ranch dressing mix. Turn the mixture out into the baking dish. Sprinkle with the bread crumbs, and drizzle with the melted butter. Bake uncovered for 50 to 60 minutes, or until the potatoes are golden brown and cooked through.

Serves 6 to 8

These fun little Green Bean Bundles are perfect for a simple family dinner but are fancy enough to serve to company. If you find the bacon isn't crisping enough, just switch on the broiler for a few minutes to get it crispy.

Preheat the oven to 400°. Lightly spray a 13 x 9-inch baking dish with nonstick cooking spray.

Drain the green beans. Lay one slice of bacon flat and slice it into quarters by cutting it both horizontally and vertically.

Take 4 to 6 green beans and wrap them with a piece of bacon; tie the bacon into a small knot. Continue to make bundles until all the green beans have been used. Place the bundles into the baking dish. In a small bowl mix the onion soup mix with 1/2 cup water, and then pour it over the bundles. Bake uncovered for 30 minutes or until the bacon is crispy.

Serves 4 to 6

2 (14 1/2-ounce) cans whole green beans

6 to 8 slices thinly sliced bacon

1 (1-ounce) package onion soup mix

1/2 cup water

This salad actually has three recipes. The Balsamic Dressing and the Candied Pecans really make the salad. Feel free to replace the strawberries and blueberries with any of your favorite fruits to change things up a bit.

In a large bowl toss the baby spinach, feta cheese crumbles, strawberries, blueberries, and candied pecans. Drizzle with the balsamic dressing right before serving.

Serves 4 to 6

SALAD:

1 (6-ounce) package baby spinach

1 (4-ounce) container feta cheese crumbles

1 cup sliced strawberries

1 cup blueberries

1 cup Candied Pecans

Balsamic Dressing

Preheat the oven to 325°. Lightly grease a baking sheet.

In a medium bowl whip the egg white and water together until frothy. Add the pecans, and toss to coat.

In another small bowl combine the sugar, salt, and cinnamon. Add to the pecans, and stir to coat. Spread the pecans out on the baking sheet, and bake 28 to 30 minutes, stirring twice during the cooking time. Be cautious not to overcook them. Cool completely. Store in an airtight container or jar for about a week.

Makes 2 cups

CANDIED PECANS:

1 large egg white

1 tablespoon water

2 cups raw pecans

1/2 cup sugar

1 teaspoon salt

1/2 teaspoon ground cinnamon

In a medium bowl whisk together the balsamic vinegar, mustard, and honey. Once combined, gradually whisk in the olive oil.

Makes about 2/3 cup

BALSAMIC DRESSING:

4 tablespoons balsamic vinegar

1 teaspoon Dijon mustard

1 tablespoon honey

1/3 cup olive oil

Squash Dressing

TRACY MOORE
WOODVILLE, ALABAMA

In the South, we love our yellow summer squash. In Tracy's family, they love their Squash Dressing. She tells me that her family demands this at every gathering. If she's not planning to attend, she's required to send it along with someone else.

3 (14 ½-ounce) cans squash with onions, drained and mashed

4 cups crumbled cornbread

1 small onion, chopped

5 large eggs

2 (10 ¾-ounce) cans cream of chicken soup

1 cup (2 sticks) butter, melted

2 cups shredded Cheddar cheese

Salt and black pepper

Preheat the oven to 350°. Grease a 13 x 9-inch baking dish.

Combine the squash, cornbread, onion, eggs, soup, butter, and cheese in a large bowl. Add salt and pepper to taste. Pour into the baking dish, and bake 35 to 40 minutes or until golden brown.

Serves 10 to 12

After years of my mom and me searching for the perfect Corn Salad recipe, we finally gave up and just developed our own. We probably should have done that in the first place. I love the green chilies in this. They aren't hot, and they provide the perfect amount of tartness and zing.

In a medium bowl combine the drained corn, onions, drained chilies, tomatoes, mayonnaise, red wine vinegar, salt, pepper, and garlic powder. Stir well. Refrigerate for at least 1 hour to allow the flavors to blend.

Serves 4 to 6

2 (11-ounce) cans white shoepeg corn, drained

4 green onions, chopped

1 (4-ounce) can chopped green chilies, drained

2 Roma tomatoes, seeded and chopped

4 tablespoons mayonnaise

2 tablespoons red wine vinegar

1/4 teaspoon salt

1/4 teaspoon black pepper

1/4 teaspoon garlic powder

Turnip Greens with Cornmeal Dumplings

Big Mama, my great-grandmother, was an amazing cook. This was one of her signature dishes. Many meals at her table were composed of this and this only. I think about that sweet, amazing little lady every time I make this.

FOR THE TURNIP GREENS:

2 quarts water

1 smoked ham hock

1 onion, coarsely chopped

2 chicken bouillon cubes

1 tablespoon salt

2 garlic cloves

1 pound washed and chopped turnip greens

In a large pot with a tight-fitting lid, add the water, ham hock, onion, bouillon cubes, salt, and garlic. Bring to a boil over medium-high heat, and then reduce to a simmer, cover, and cook 1 hour.

Add the turnip greens; cover, and cook an additional 45 minutes, stirring occasionally.

FOR THE DUMPLINGS:

1 cup self-rising cornmeal

$1/2$ teaspoon salt

$2/3$ cup water

In a small bowl combine the cornmeal, salt, and water. Stir until mixed well. Return the turnips to a rolling boil over medium-high heat. Remove the lid, and drop teaspoonsful of the dumpling batter into the boiling liquid. Do not stir. Return the lid to the pot, and cook an additional 10 to 15 minutes without stirring or removing the lid.

Serves 4 to 6

No Southern picnic, barbecue, or family reunion is complete without at least two different kinds of potato salad. This is the way my mom makes it. My favorite way to eat it is while it's still warm. Mom would always spoon me out some in a separate bowl so I could have a snack before dinner. For added flavor, sprinkle the potatoes with a little white vinegar right after you drain them.

Wash, peel, and cut the potatoes into 3/4-inch cubes. Place the potatoes in a medium-size pot, and cover them with water. Add the salt, and heat to boiling over medium-high heat. Then reduce the heat to a simmer, and cook 15 to 20 minutes or until the potatoes are tender but not mushy. Drain the potatoes well.

In a large bowl combine the chopped eggs, onion, mustard, mayo, and pickle relish. Stir until well mixed. Add the drained potatoes, and toss gently to coat. Refrigerate until served.

Serves about 4

1 ½ pounds baking potatoes

1 teaspoon salt

3 large hard-boiled eggs, peeled and finely chopped

½ small sweet onion, finely chopped

2 teaspoons prepared mustard

½ cup mayonnaise

3 tablespoons dill pickle relish

There was rarely a summer meal growing up that didn't have tomatoes somewhere on the table. Sometimes they were served with just a little salt and black pepper. This recipe is one of my parents' favorite ways to take advantage of the abundance of garden-fresh tomatoes they grow every year.

4 medium garden fresh
  tomatoes

3/4 cup mayonnaise

1 sleeve saltine crackers,
  coarsely broken

Seed and coarsely chop the tomatoes. In a medium bowl combine the tomatoes and mayonnaise. Add the broken crackers and lightly toss. Serve immediately.

Serves 4 to 5

Indulgent Macaroni and Cheese

MISTY CORRALES
BIRMINGHAM, ALABAMA

For Misty, and many other folks, macaroni and cheese is the ultimate comfort food. Her grandfather made the best. She has fond memories of his version of the dish, but didn't have his recipe to recreate the masterpiece. For years, she's been perfecting the recipe to find something close to his. And while she claims that it's not exact, it's close enough to remind her of him every time she makes it.

Preheat the oven to 350°. Grease a 13 x 9-inch baking dish.

Cook the macaroni according to the package directions; then drain and return it to the pot over low heat. Add the margarine, and stir until it is melted. Add the Cheddar cheese, gorgonzola, mozzarella, and 1 cup of the Colby Jack cheese. Stir until the cheeses are combined and almost melted.

In another medium bowl combine the egg whites, milk, sour cream, and dry mustard. Add the egg mixture to the pot, and stir well to combine. Add salt and pepper to taste. Pour the mixture into the baking dish. Bake 35 minutes. Carefully add the remaining 1 cup of Colby Jack cheese, and return the dish to the oven until the cheese has melted.

Serves 8 to 10

4 cups uncooked elbow macaroni

1/4 (1/2 stick) margarine

2 cups shredded Cheddar cheese

1/2 cup gorgonzola cheese

1 cup shredded mozzarella cheese

2 cups shredded Colby Jack cheese, divided

4 large egg whites

1 cup milk

1/2 cup sour cream

1 tablespoon dry mustard

Salt and black pepper

Succotash is an inexpensive dish that became immensely popular during the Great Depression because of its frugality. I like this dish for the same reason and because of all the great flavor that comes out of it.

6 slices bacon, coarsely chopped

1 medium onion, chopped

1 small green bell pepper, seeded and chopped

3 cloves garlic, minced

1 cup chicken broth

1 (16-ounce) package frozen lima beans

1 (14 1/2-ounce) can diced tomatoes

1 (16-ounce) package frozen whole kernel corn

1 cup cut okra

In a large skillet over medium heat, cook the chopped bacon until crispy. Drain away all but about 2 table-spoons of the bacon grease, then return the pan to the heat. Add the onion and bell pepper, and cook 7 to 8 minutes or until the onions are translucent. Add the garlic, and cook 1 minute. Stir in the chicken broth and lima beans. Cook 8 to 10 minutes, stirring occasionally. Stir in the tomatoes with juice, corn, and okra. Cover, and cook 15 to 20 minutes or until the vegetables are cooked to your liking.

Serves 6 to 8

BACON FRIED RICE

I love fried rice, but don't have much luck making it at home. It always ends up mushy and lacks flavor. That is until I tried it this way. The recipe was inspired by an old friend of mine, and I just tweaked it to put my special touch on it.

1/2 pound (6 to 8 slices) bacon

8 green onions, chopped

4 cups cold cooked white rice*

3 cloves garlic, minced

3 tablespoons soy sauce

In a large nonstick skillet cook the bacon over medium heat until crispy. Remove and drain the bacon on paper towels, then crumble. Add the onion to the bacon grease, and continue to cook over medium heat for 3 to 4 minutes. Increase the heat to medium-high, and add the cold rice and garlic. Cook 6 to 8 minutes, stirring frequently, or until the rice is heated through. Add the crumbled bacon and soy sauce, stir well, and serve.

Serves about 4

* All my previous attempts at fried rice failed because I didn't use cold rice. That's really the trick here.

Green Beans Braised with Onions

ANNE McKEOWN
JACKSON, MISSISSIPPI

In Anne's search to add something besides the ubiquitous green bean casserole to their holiday menu, she ran across this recipe in the newspaper some twenty years ago. Though the actual recipe has long since disappeared, the dish returns to their table every year.

Melt the butter in a medium saucepan over medium heat, and add the onions. Cook until the onions begin to turn golden. Add the green beans, chicken broth, and rosemary. Cover the pan and cook about 15 minutes or until the beans are tender. Remove the lid and continue cooking until most of the liquid has evaporated. Add salt and pepper to taste.

Serves 4 to 6

¼ cup (½ stick) butter

2 small onions, thinly sliced

2 pounds fresh green beans, washed and trimmed

¼ cup chicken broth

Sprig of fresh rosemary

Salt and black pepper

I'll admit that Brussels sprouts can be an acquired taste. Most folks don't know that the flavor actually gets stronger the more you cook them. So my advice is that if you cook them less, you might like them more. Put away the memory of those mushy overcooked sprouts from your childhood, and give these a try.

Wash the Brussels sprouts, and remove the outer leaves. Cut them in half.

In a large skillet over medium heat, add the chopped bacon and cook until slightly crispy. Add the butter, and melt it completely. Add the onion, garlic, and Brussels sprouts, and cook about 10 minutes or until the sprouts are tender, stirring occasionally. Add salt and pepper to taste.

Serves 4 to 6

1 pound Brussels sprouts

5 slices bacon, coarsely chopped

2 tablespoons butter

1/2 large onion, chopped

2 cloves garlic, minced

1/2 teaspoon salt

1/2 teaspoon black pepper

SPICY BLACK-EYED PEAS

I love black-eyed peas, but I can get a little bored with the same old flavor. This recipe takes advantage of a can of tomatoes with green chilies to add some spice and flavor. Feel free to use the hot or mild ones depending on your own taste buds.

2 tablespoons butter

1 medium onion, chopped

2 cloves garlic, minced

4 cups water

1 (16-ounce) package dried
  black-eyed peas

1 teaspoon salt

1/2 teaspoon black pepper

1 chicken bouillon cube

1 (10-ounce) can diced
  tomatoes with green chilies

In a large pot or Dutch oven with a tight-fitting lid, heat the butter over medium heat. Once melted, add the onion and cook 7 to 8 minutes or until the onion is translucent. Add the garlic, and cook about 1 minute. Stir in the water, black-eyed peas, salt, pepper, bouillon cube, and tomatoes with the juice. Stir well, reduce the heat to a simmer, cover, and cook 45 minutes to 1 hour, adding additional water if necessary.

Serves about 8

Best-Ever Rice and Mushrooms

MARGARET EICHLER
INDIANAPOLIS, INDIANA

Margaret was afraid this recipe was going to be "too simple" for me to include. She obviously doesn't know me very well. I don't think there is even such a thing as "too simple." She also says this recipe doubles easily, and trust me, based on how good this tastes, doubling this one is something you might want to do.

Melt the butter in a medium saucepan with a tight-fitting lid. Add the French onion soup and mushrooms with the liquid. Bring the mixture to a boil. Add the rice, and stir once. Cover immediately, and reduce the heat to the lowest setting. Cook 25 minutes without stirring. Remove from the heat, and let stand for 10 minutes without removing the lid.

Fluff the rice with a fork and serve.

Serves 4 to 6

1/4 cup (1/2 stick) butter

1 (10 1/2-ounce) can French onion soup

1 (8-ounce) can mushrooms

1 cup parboiled long-grain rice

Where I'm From . . .

Where I'm from isn't just a geographical location; it's a state of mind. It's found somewhere between sweet tea and fried okra—to the left of the billowing Spanish moss, sandwiched smack-dab in the middle of *please* and *thank you*.

We hold doors for one another. We do that not only because it's the nice thing to do but also because our mamas would slap the backs of our heads if we didn't.

Down here we celebrate everything with food. New neighbors, babies, birthdays, sickness, and death are all met with casserole-carrying folks eager to offer congratulations or condolences—whichever it might be.

Where I'm from we say, "Yes, ma'am" and "No, ma'am" and "Yes, sir" and "No, sir" regardless of the age of the person we're addressing.

Down here the drawls are sweet and slow like sorghum molasses. We have special words that only we Southerners are allowed to use, like *fixin'* and *y'all.*

No, we don't all drive tractors and live on farms. We aren't all lucky enough for that.

Where I'm from you'll find folks pulled over on the side of the road to allow a funeral procession to pass.

Where I'm from is a place that is filled with folks who live a life of gratitude. We appreciate everything from the amazing breath in our lungs to the way the moonlight glimmers on the water of the passing river.

Down here food is like currency too. It's only south of the Mason-Dixon Line that you still find professional folks like doctors, hairstylists, and lawyers getting repaid with a bunch of greens or a couple jars of homemade jelly.

No, we're not all rednecks, but some of the most fun I've ever had was with folks who claimed to be ones.

You won't pass a man in a pickup truck on a back-country road and not get a smile, a nod, or a wave.

Where I come from is not just a place. It's a feeling, an idea, a lifestyle. What a world it would be if we were all lucky enough to be from where I'm from.

POTLUCK BITES

WHETHER IT'S A FAMILY REUNION, A COMPANY PICNIC, A CHURCH supper, or even a funeral, the potluck is a popular event south of the Mason-Dixon Line. One of the things I enjoy the most about potluck isn't the food. Sure, I'm all for a big spread, but you never know what kinds of things might show up. We all have those "fringe" family members who will make a gelatin mold out of anything or the one whose dish you are positive you saw cat hair in. In my family, most of us know whose dishes to avoid, but it became an issue when my wife began attending family events with us. She hadn't had the same experiences we'd had, so I had her follow me and take only from the dishes I dipped from. You know exactly what I'm talking about.

But I digress. Potluck in my family is also about preserving recipes that always make an appearance regardless of whether the family member who made it famous is still around or not. It might be Big Mama's Turnip Greens with Cornmeal Dumplings or Great Aunt Betty's Skillet Cake. By keeping their recipes on the table, we just keep those folks right there with us.

Hash Brown Casserole

You just about can't attend a potluck in the South and not see some form of Hash Brown Casserole mixed in among the brightly colored baking dishes. You might even locate a couple varieties. This is a recipe from my wife's side of the family that we've been using for years. It's always a hit when we show up with it.

1 (26- to 32-ounce) bag frozen shredded hash brown potatoes

1/2 medium onion, finely chopped

1 (8-ounce) bag shredded sharp Cheddar cheese

1 (8-ounce) container sour cream

1 (10 3/4-ounce) can cream of chicken soup

1 teaspoon salt

1/2 teaspoon garlic powder

1/3 cup plain bread crumbs

1/2 cup (1 stick) butter, melted

Preheat the oven to 350°. Grease a 13 x 9-inch baking dish.

In a large bowl combine the hash browns, onion, Cheddar cheese, sour cream, cream of chicken, salt, and garlic powder. Stir to mix well. Spread the mixture into the baking dish. Sprinkle with the bread crumbs, and drizzle with the melted butter. Bake 1 hour and 10 minutes or until bubbly and golden brown.

Serves 6 to 8

POPPY SEED CHICKEN CASSEROLE

I have a confession. I had never had Poppy Seed Chicken Casserole until my wife made it for me after we married. She loves the stuff, and together we developed this simple recipe that packs a lot more flavor than some other recipes we've tried. Many folks use cream of chicken, but we prefer the cream of mushroom because of the added flavor.

Preheat the oven to 350°. Lightly grease a 13 x 9-inch baking dish.

In a large bowl combine the chicken, mushroom soup, sour cream, garlic powder, poppy seeds, and salt and pepper to taste. Pour the mixture into the baking dish. Top with the crushed crackers, and drizzle with the melted butter. Bake 30 minutes or until hot and bubbly. Serve over white rice.

Serves 4 to 6

3 cups chopped, cooked chicken

1 (10 3/4-ounce) can cream of mushroom soup

1 (16-ounce) container sour cream

1/2 teaspoon garlic powder

1 tablespoon poppy seeds

Salt and black pepper

1 sleeve buttery round crackers, crushed

1/4 cup (1/2 stick) butter, melted

Cooked hot white rice

This is another recipe that has been immensely popular on the blog. Cooking it in a slow cooker really makes the process a lot easier and less messy. You'll be amazed too, once you see how easy it is to make these simple homemade dumplings.

2 tablespoons butter

2 (10 3/4-ounce) cans cream of chicken soup

1 (14 1/2-ounce) can chicken broth

1 cup water

1 small onion, chopped

4 boneless, skinless chicken breasts

1/2 cup self-rising flour

5 tablespoons ice-cold water

Add the butter, chicken soup, chicken broth, water, onions, and chicken breasts to the bowl of a 4-quart slow cooker. Make sure the breasts are covered with liquid, add additional water if necessary. Cover and cook on low for 6 to 8 hours.

About an hour before serving, turn the slow cooker up to high and shred your chicken using two forks. In a small bowl combine the self-rising flour with ice-cold water. You may have to add a little more water or a little more flour to get to the right consistency to roll out. Turn the dough out onto a floured surface, and roll thin (about 1/8 inch). Cut the dough into 1-inch squares with a pizza cutter or knife. Drop the dumplings around the edge of the slow cooker where it is the hottest, and stir gently. Be sure the dumplings are covered with liquid. Cover and cook at least 45 minutes more.

Serves about 4

Slow cooking chili gives it a rich, deep flavor that can't compare to any package mix. The slow cooker is the perfect vessel for chili because it's a low-maintenance way to get that bold flavor without having to be in the kitchen all day.

In the bowl of a 4-quart slow cooker, add the ground beef, stew meat, onion, bell pepper, kidney beans, petite diced tomatoes, diced tomatoes with chilies, beef broth, tomato paste, chili powder, cumin, ranch dressing mix, and garlic. Stir well and cover; cook on low for 8 hours, stirring only once or twice.

Serves 6 to 8

- 1 pound ground beef, browned and drained
- 1 pound beef stew meat, cubed
- 1 onion, chopped
- 1 green bell pepper, seeded and chopped
- 1 (15 1/2-ounce) can kidney beans, drained and rinsed
- 1 (14 1/2-ounce) can petite diced tomatoes, undrained
- 1 (10-ounce) can diced tomatoes with green chilies, undrained
- 1 (14 1/2-ounce) can beef broth
- 1 (6-ounce) can tomato paste
- 3 teaspoons chili powder
- 2 teaspoons ground cumin
- 1 (1.0-ounce) package ranch dressing mix
- 3 garlic cloves, peeled and smashed

SOUTHERN LAYERED SALAD

I bet there are 47,873 different ways to assemble a layered salad—maybe even more. The ingredients and dressings might vary, but the end result is always yummy. Here's my take.

Add the lettuce to the bottom of a large bowl, and lightly pack it down. Next, layer the celery, sweet peas, bacon, red onion, bell pepper, and Cheddar cheese. In a small bowl combine the mayonnaise and sugar. Spread it over the top of the salad. Cover and refrigerate for up to 8 hours.

Serves 6 to 8

1 small head iceberg lettuce, chopped

2 ribs celery, chopped

1 (8 1/2-ounce) can sweet peas, drained

8 slices crispy cooked bacon, crumbled (about 1/2 cup)

1 small red onion, chopped

1 green bell pepper, seeded and chopped

2 cups shredded Cheddar cheese

2 cups mayonnaise

2 teaspoons sugar

Louise Rogers's Chicken Spaghetti

CONNIE ROGERS
NORTHPORT, ALABAMA

I spent the first three years of my life in the tiny town of Camden, Alabama, and my grandparents still live there. When I saw a recipe from a reader whose mother-in-law was from Camden, it was nearly a shoo-in. It's truly an honor to be able to share Louise's recipe with the world. I'm told she would make huge batches of it and freeze it so she would have it on hand for get-togethers, church suppers and to take to friends in times of illness or tragedy.

1 (5 to 6-pound) chicken

1 (16-ounce) package spaghetti

1 cup butter

3 large onions, chopped

2 large green bell peppers, chopped

1 (8-ounce) can mushrooms, drained (optional)

1 (15-ounce) can sweet peas, drained

2 (14 1/2-ounce) cans petite diced tomatoes

5 tablespoons Worcestershire sauce

2 (10 3/4-ounce) cans condensed tomato soup

2 1/2 cups water

1 (16-ounce) package shredded sharp Cheddar cheese

1 (3.8-ounce) can sliced olives (optional)

Add the chicken to a large stock pot, and just cover with water. Heat over medium-low, cooking 40 to 50 minutes or until the chicken is cooked through. Carefully remove the chicken and cool. Increase the heat to medium-high, and add the spaghetti to the stock once it reaches a boil. Cook according to the instructions on the spaghetti package to reach an al dente doneness. Drain the spaghetti, and set it aside. Remove the meat from the chicken and shred it.

Preheat the oven to 350°. Grease a very large baking dish.

Turn the heat down to medium, and return the stock pot to the stovetop. Add the butter, onions, and bell peppers, and cook 7 to 8 minutes or until the vegetables are tender. Return the shredded chicken to the pot, and add the mushrooms, peas, diced tomatoes with the juice, Worcestershire sauce, tomato soup, and water. Cook on medium low, stirring frequently,

35 to 45 minutes or until the liquid has reduced. Add the drained spaghetti to the pot, and stir well. Pour the mixture into the baking dish, and top with the cheese and olives. Bake 30 to 35 minutes or until the casserole is hot and bubbly.

If desired, the casserole can be divided between 3 to 4 smaller baking dishes before being baked and then frozen. To reheat, cook in a 350° oven until the casserole is heated through; then add the cheese and olives and return to the oven until hot and bubbly.

Serves 16 to 18

BACON AND BLUE BROCCOLI SALAD

Bacon and blue cheese is a common flavor pairing that appears in everything from burgers to salad dressings. This grown-up version of broccoli salad is always popular, and it's one of my favorite picnic sides.

1 large bunch broccoli, washed and chopped (about 5 cups)

1 medium red onion, chopped

1 (4-ounce) container blue cheese crumbles

5 slices crispy cooked bacon, crumbled (about 1/3 cup)

1 cup mayonnaise

2 tablespoons cider vinegar

Salt and black pepper

In a large bowl combine the broccoli, onion, blue cheese, and bacon. In a small bowl combine the mayonnaise and cider vinegar. Add the dressing to the broccoli, and toss to coat. Add salt and pepper to taste. Refrigerate at least 1 hour to allow the flavors to blend.

Serves 4 to 5

As with so many of my recipes, you are welcome to substitute fresh ingredients for the canned or frozen ones listed. You'll just have to adjust the cooking time accordingly. This recipe is a great example of that. Just swap the canned tomatoes for fresh ones that have been seeded and chopped, and add ten to fifteen minutes to the baking time.

Preheat the oven to 350°. Grease an 8 x 8-inch baking dish. Drain the tomatoes very well in a large mesh strainer.

In a medium skillet melt the butter over medium-low heat. Add the onion, and cook 7 to 8 minutes or until the onions are translucent. Add the garlic, and cook 2 minutes. Pour the onions and garlic into a large bowl. To the bowl add the drained tomatoes, egg, cheese, salt, pepper, and dried basil. Mix well, and pour the mixture into the baking dish. Top with the crushed crackers, and bake 20 to 25 minutes or until hot and bubbly.

Serves 4 to 5

- 1 (28-ounce) can diced tomatoes
- 1 tablespoon butter
- 1/2 small onion, chopped
- 2 garlic cloves, minced
- 1 large egg
- 1 cup Italian blend shredded cheese
- 1/2 teaspoon salt
- 1/4 teaspoon black pepper
- 1/2 teaspoon dried basil
- 20 buttery round crackers, crushed

Slow Cooker White Beans

The smoky flavor that these beans have is really what makes them special. They are perfect served alongside a big piece of crusty, hot cornbread.

In the bowl of a 4- to 5-quart slow cooker, combine the dried beans, ham, onion, water, salt, and pepper. Stir, cover, and cook on low for 6 to 8 hours or until the beans have reached your desired tenderness.

Serves 6 to 8

1 (16-ounce) package dried Great Northern Beans

1 pound smoked ham hocks or ham pieces

1 small onion, chopped

6 cups water

2 teaspoons salt

1/2 teaspoon black pepper

Pineapple Cheese Casserole

SUSAN HATCHER
MILLEDGEVILLE, GEORGIA

Susan has been one of my most loyal blog followers. I bet she's been there from the very beginning, offering love and support and sharing her recipes. This recipe of hers is one of my wife's most favorite sides. She loves the sweet and salty combination.

1 cup sugar

6 tablespoons all-purpose flour

1 (20-ounce) can crushed pineapple, drained

2 cups shredded sharp Cheddar cheese

2 cups crushed buttery round crackers

6 tablespoons butter, melted

Preheat the oven to 350°. Grease an 8 x 8-inch baking dish.

In a large bowl mix the sugar and flour. Add the pineapple and cheese, and stir to combine. Pour the mixture into the baking dish. Top with the crushed crackers, and drizzle with the melted butter. Bake 30 to 35 minutes or until hot and bubbly.

Serves 4 to 5

SLOW COOKER RED BEANS AND RICE

In some parts of the South, Monday is traditionally Red Beans and Rice day. That day was set aside as wash day, so while the clothes were being washed, you could put a big pot of red beans on to cook without having to spend much time watching them. In my family, it seems like every day is wash day, but we still love a big pot of Slow Cooker Red Beans and Rice every now and then. This recipe works great in a slow cooker because you don't have an untended pot rumbling away on the stove. You can just turn it on and let it go.

Sort and rinse the beans as directed on the package. In the bowl of a 4-quart slow cooker, combine the beans, sausage, ham hock, celery, bell pepper, onion, garlic, water, and salt, and stir well. Cover and cook on low for 5 to 6 hours or until the beans are done to your liking. Serve over hot white rice.

Serves 6 to 8

1 pound dried red beans

1 pound Cajun smoked sausage, cut into 1-inch pieces

1 smoked ham hock

3 ribs celery, chopped

1 green bell pepper, chopped

1 large onion, chopped

4 garlic cloves, shopped

8 cups water

2 teaspoons salt

Cooked hot white rice

This is a great all-purpose vegetable casserole that is perfect with just about any family meal or potluck. It's also pretty versatile in that you can switch the green beans and corn out for other canned varieties of your favorite vegetables.

2 tablespoons butter

1 small onion, chopped

2 ribs celery, thinly sliced

1 (14 1/2-ounce) can French-style green beans, drained

1 (11-ounce) can shoepeg corn, drained

1 (10 1/2-ounce) can cream of celery soup

1/2 cup sour cream

3/4 cup shredded Cheddar cheese

1/2 teaspoon salt

1/2 teaspoon black pepper

16 buttery round crackers

Preheat the oven to 350°. Grease a 1 1/2-quart baking dish.

In a medium skillet melt the butter over medium heat. Add the onion and celery. Cook until the onion is translucent and just starting to brown on the edges, about 10 minutes.

In a large bowl combine the cooked onion and celery with the drained green beans and corn. Add the cream of celery soup, sour cream, Cheddar cheese, salt, and pepper. Stir to combine. Pour into the baking dish. Crumble the buttery crackers on top. Bake 30 to 35 minutes or until the casserole is bubbly.

Serves 6 to 8

CHEESY CORN AND RICE CASSEROLE

This super simple casserole is the perfect side for any meal. Whether it's a summer barbecue, a Thanksgiving buffet, or even a springtime church supper, this dish is sure to fit the bill.

Preheat the oven to 350°. Grease an 8 x 8-inch baking dish. Cook the rice according to package directions.

Combine the cooked rice, cream of chicken soup, corn, and butter. Pour into the baking dish. Bake 20 to 30 minutes or until bubbly. Remove from the oven, top with the cheese, and return to the oven until the cheese is melted.

Serves 4 to 5

1 (5-ounce) package yellow rice mix

1 (10 3/4-ounce) can cream of chicken soup

1 (15 1/4-ounce) can whole kernel corn, drained

1 tablespoon butter, melted

1 cup shredded Cheddar cheese

Slow Cooker Beef Stew

I love using my slow cooker. In fact, I've developed a bit of an obsession as a result. While most folks make do with just one, I've got five slow cookers of varying sizes. I've got one for small things like dips. One I use when I'm cooking for just the three of us. One I use for larger meals like soups and stews. Well, you get the picture.

Salt and black pepper

2 pounds beef stew meat

1/3 cup all-purpose flour

3 tablespoons vegetable oil

5 potatoes, peeled and chopped

4 carrots, peeled and chopped

3 ribs celery, chopped

1 small onion, chopped

4 cups beef broth

1 teaspoon garlic powder

2 (0.87-ounce) packages brown gravy mix

In a large bowl generously salt and pepper the meat. Add the flour, and toss with the meat until coated.

Heat the oil in a large skillet over medium heat. Add the meat, and cook in batches if necessary until it is just browned. Remove the meat from the pan, and set aside.

In the slow cooker bowl, place the potatoes on the bottom, top with the carrots, celery, and browned meat; then add onions. In a small bowl combine the beef broth and garlic powder with the gravy packages. Pour the mixture into the crock. Cover and cook on low for 7 to 8 hours, stirring once in the last hour.

Serves about 4

MACARONI SALAD

After a tragic childhood incident at a family reunion that included an unidentified, foul-tasting, gooey gelatin mess from Aunt So-and-So, I've been a little apprehensive about potlucks. Sometimes it takes only one time to get burned. For me, one thing that is usually pretty safe, though, is the conventional Macaroni Salad. It's a safe and delicious dish that even your most skeptical relative will love.

3 cups uncooked elbow macaroni

1 cup mayonnaise

1 tablespoon prepared mustard

3 tablespoons white vinegar

1/2 teaspoon black pepper

2 teaspoons sugar

1 teaspoon salt

1/2 teaspoon garlic powder

1/2 teaspoon onion powder

1 small red onion, finely chopped

1 stalk celery, finely chopped

1/2 green bell pepper, seeded and finely chopped

Cook the macaroni according to package directions and drain. In a small bowl stir together the mayonnaise, mustard, vinegar, pepper, sugar, salt, garlic powder, and onion powder.

In a large bowl combine the macaroni, onion, celery, and bell pepper. Add the dressing, and stir to combine. Refrigerate for at least 2 hours to allow the flavors to blend.

Serves 4 to 6

Mary's Jambalaya

KIM BOX
PRATTVILLE, ALABAMA

When Kim's son was born, her dear friend Mary showed up with this delicious dish. (See, I told you we Southerners celebrate everything with food!) One bite, and she just had to have the recipe. Anytime Kim now shows up with this jambalaya, she always gets asked for the recipe.

Preheat the oven to 350°. In a large roasting pan with a tight-fitting lid, add the sausage, chicken or shrimp, consommé, soup, tomato sauce, butter, bell pepper, parsley, rice, garlic powder, and Creole seasoning. Stir to combine. Cover, and bake 1 hour and 15 minutes, stirring every 20 minutes or so.

Serves 8 to 10

2 pounds hot smoked sausage, sliced

2 pounds chicken breasts, chopped (or 2 pounds raw shrimp, peeled)

1 (10 3/4-ounce) can beef consommé

1 (10 1/2-ounce) can French onion soup

1 (15-ounce) can tomato sauce

1/2 cup (1 stick) butter

1 large bell pepper, seeded and chopped (your choice of color)

4 tablespoons chopped parsley

1 (1-pound) box parboiled rice

1 teaspoon garlic powder

1 tablespoon Creole seasoning

Slow Cooker Pot Roast

One of the best things about slow-cooker meals is being able to drop everything into the crock and come home eight hours later to a house filled with the wonderful smells of a meal that is ready to eat. Once I started doing my pot roast and vegetables in the slow cooker, I abandoned the more time-consuming oven method that always heated up the kitchen.

1 (4- to 5-pound) beef chuck roast

3 garlic cloves, peeled

1 1/2 cups baby carrots

3 ribs celery, coarsely chopped

5 medium potatoes, cut into 1-inch chunks

1 medium onion, coarsely chopped

1/4 cup soy sauce

1 cup beef broth

1 (10 3/4-ounce) can cream of mushroom soup

1/4 teaspoon black pepper

Place the roast in the bowl of a 4-quart slow cooker. Add the garlic, carrots, celery, potatoes, and onion.

In a small bowl combine the soy sauce, broth, mushroom soup, and pepper. Pour over the vegetables and roast. Cover, and cook 7 to 8 hours on low.

Serves 4

CHICKEN AND DUMPLINGS CASSEROLE

I'll never forget the first time my mom told me she was making Chicken and Dumplings Casserole. I was a little afraid of what I was in for, but I knew, regardless, that it wasn't going to taste anything like traditional Chicken and Dumplings. Boy, was I wrong! This has all the great flavor of Chicken and Dumplings but without all the work.

Preheat the oven to 350°. In a large skillet over medium heat, melt the butter. Add the chopped onion and celery, and cook 8 to 10 minutes. Pour the mixture into the bottom of a 13 x 9-inch baking dish. Add the chicken in a layer on top of the vegetables.

In a small bowl mix the flour and milk together. Pour the mixture over the chicken. In another small bowl, combine the broth, cream of chicken soup, salt, and pepper. Pour it over the chicken. Do not mix the layers. Bake 40 to 45 minutes or until the casserole is set.

Serves 6 to 8

1/2 cup (1 stick) butter

1 small onion, chopped

2 ribs celery, chopped

3 cups cooked, shredded chicken

1 cup self-rising flour

1 cup milk

2 cups chicken broth

1 (10 3/4-ounce) cream of chicken soup

1/2 teaspoon salt

1/4 teaspoon black pepper

Why Christmas Trees Don't Have to Be Green

MY GRANDMOTHER GREW UP POOR. SHE WAS ONE OF SIX CHILDREN. Out of necessity, both her parents worked to make ends meet, which left her older siblings to raise her. That was common in those days. Her father was a night watchman at a saw mill, and her mother worked at a plant nursery.

When Christmas would roll around, though, poverty took nothing from them in the way of holiday magic and excitement. The holidays were always a very special time for them. Every year each child would be presented with one toy, a homemade outfit, and a small assortment of fruit, nuts, and peppermint candies. That was a big Christmas to them.

As part of their Christmas tradition, it was always her father's job to go out and hunt for the perfect Christmas tree. That was his big contribution to the celebration, and he took great pride in presenting the perfect cedar tree for trimming. Of course, running down to the tree lot was out of the budget, so he would set out into the woods to track down a prime specimen. One year in particular, he wasn't able to find a cedar tree to suit. After hours of searching, in a last-ditch effort to provide something, he cut down a small holly bush he found. Back at home, feeling a little embarrassed with his haul, he set out to make the puny bush special. Finding a can of silver paint, he painstakingly brushed every single prickly holly leaf with a shiny coat. They added the few ornaments they had and one small strand of bubble lights they had saved for months to buy.

The result, as my grandmother would put it, was the most beautiful, amazing Christmas tree she's ever had. It wasn't about it being the perfect size or color, or even about it being a tree at all. The love he put into that tree is what made it beautiful. That particular tree went down in history with her and her family. The thing that he thought inadequate became the main focus of one of the fondest Christmases they ever shared.

Hearing my grandmother tell this story when I was a child, I remember trying to figure out how someone could be so excited about a silver bush and only one toy for Christmas. She would reflect on Christmases past with the same starry-eyed look that I'm sure she had when she was four years old.

Today, as an adult with my own child, I have a much better understanding of the importance of a simple but impactful holiday. So often we get caught up in the holiday season that we fail to realize the simple things that make it so special. We focus our attention on buying the best gifts and decorating the perfect tree, when the real importance of the holiday lies in sharing time with our loved ones.

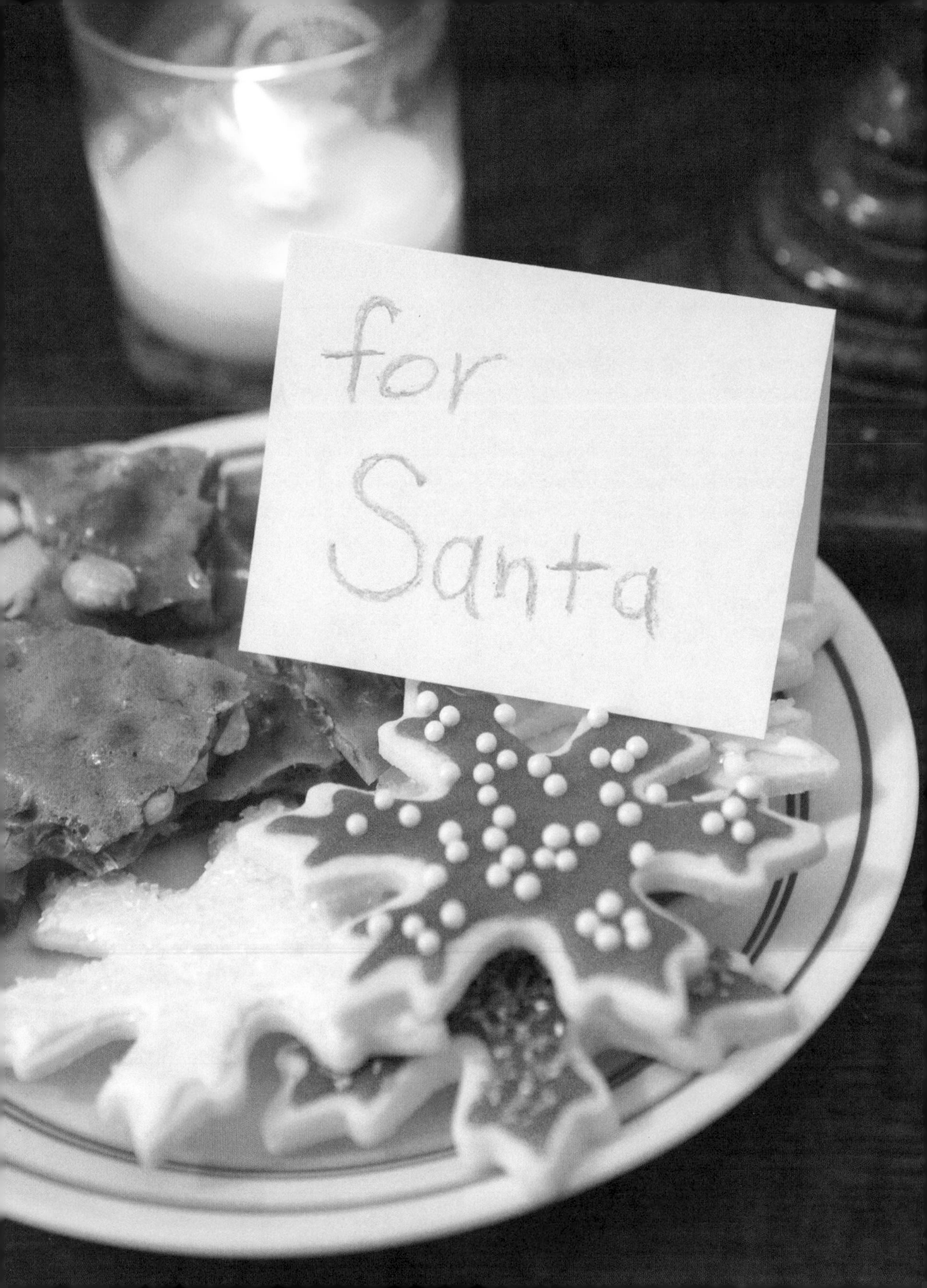
for
Santa

Holiday Bites

SOME OF MY FONDEST MEMORIES OF MY FAMILY HAVE US GATHERED around the table during the holidays. We've always been big on celebrating, and like many folks, the holidays give us an opportunity to stop and take note of how blessed we are. We have lots of traditions in my family at the holidays too. For instance, we don't put baby Jesus in the nativity set until Christmas morning. Santa always leaves giant peppermint sticks. We always read 'Twas the Night Before Christmas on Christmas Eve. Some of our traditions have deep-rooted meanings like with the nativity set; others we just do because we've always done them.

One of the traditions that I enjoy the most is when my family gathers for Christmas cookie and candy making. We spend the whole day cooking, baking, snacking, and listening to Christmas music. It's an opportunity to take refuge from the hustle and bustle of the holiday season and just be together. Sometimes it seems like we lose focus on what the holiday season is really about. And though it may happen by accident, when we are gathered together to cook and spend time together, it always recharges my batteries and makes me turn away from the gifts and the lights and the commercialism, and just be grateful.

SOUTHERN CORNBREAD DRESSING

Growing up, it was always my job to taste the dressing every Thanksgiving to make sure it had enough salt and pepper before it went into the oven. I'd find a big spoon and scoop out a mouthful of the delicious soupy mess. I just love it that way. I'll never forget the first time my aunt saw me do it. She thought I had lost my mind. Now that she's tasted it that way, though, each year we race to see who gets the first bite once it's all mixed together.

6 cups crumbled cornbread
(about a 9-inch skillet full)

1 (10 1/2-ounce) can cream of
celery soup

1 (10 1/2-ounce) can cream of
chicken soup

1 1/2 cups chicken broth

6 green onions, chopped

Salt and black pepper

Preheat the oven to 350°. Lightly grease a 2 1/2-quart baking dish.

In a large bowl combine the cornbread, cream of celery soup, cream of chicken soup, broth, and green onions. Add salt and pepper to taste. Pour the mixture into the baking dish. Cook uncovered for 25 to 30 minutes or until golden brown.

Serves 6 to 8

I learned several years ago that one trick to delivering a great-tasting, juicy turkey is brining it. While it might seem a daunting task, it's actually pretty easy. The real challenge is just finding enough room in the refrigerator to keep it cold. I've been brining my turkeys ever since. An overnight soak in this liquid followed by your favorite cooking method should make your bird extra special.

In an extra-large stock pot combine the water, salt, sugar, garlic, soy sauce, and Italian herb seasoning. Stir until the sugar and salt have dissolved. Submerge the turkey in the brine, and refrigerate for 18 to 24 hours.

Prior to cooking, remove the turkey from brine, rinse it well with cool water to remove the excess salt, and pat it dry with paper towels. Cook the turkey as you normally would.

Makes enough brine for a 12- to 15-pound turkey

2 gallons water

1 cup salt

1 cup sugar

1 head garlic, sliced crosswise

1 1/4 cups (10 ounces) soy sauce

1 tablespoon dried Italian herb seasoning

12- to 15-pound turkey, rinsed well, with the giblets removed

The sweet and crunchy praline topping is really the star of this dish. While there seem to be two basic versions of the dish—one topped like this and another topped with roasted marshmallows—this is the way my mother has made it for years.

Preheat the oven to 350°. Grease a 1 1/2-quart baking dish.

Peel and slice the potatoes, place them in a medium saucepan, and just cover them with water. Cook over medium heat for 15 to 20 minutes or until fork-tender.

Drain the potatoes, and pour them into a large mixing bowl. Mash them well with a potato masher or a hand mixer. Add the sugar, vanilla, eggs, evaporated milk, and butter, and mix very well. Pour the mixture into the baking dish.

FOR THE SWEET POTATOES:

3 pounds medium sweet potatoes

1 1/2 cups sugar

1 teaspoon vanilla extract

2 large eggs

4 ounces evaporated milk

1/4 cup (1/2 stick) butter, softened

Combine the brown sugar, flour, butter, and pecans in a medium bowl. Spoon the mixture over the potatoes. Bake 30 to 40 minutes.

Serves 6 to 8

FOR THE TOPPING:

1 cup firmly packed light brown sugar

1/3 cup all-purpose flour

1/3 cup butter, melted

3/4 cup coarsely chopped pecans

Green Bean Casserole

While my Green Bean Casserole is pretty close to the traditional one with the cream of mushroom soup, the addition of the almonds gives it a crunch that my family and I really enjoy.

3 (14 1/2-ounce) cans cut green beans, drained

1 (10 3/4-ounce) can cream of mushroom soup

1/2 cup sour cream

1 tablespoon soy sauce

1 teaspoon garlic powder

1 teaspoon onion powder

1/4 teaspoon black pepper

1 1/2 cups French fried onions

1/2 cup slivered almonds

Preheat the oven to 350°. Grease a 13 x 9-inch baking dish.

In a large bowl combine the drained green beans, cream of mushroom soup, sour cream, soy sauce, garlic powder, onion powder, and pepper. Pour the mixture into the baking dish.

Bake 30 to 35 minutes or until bubbly. Remove the dish from the oven, and top with the fried onions and almonds. Return to the oven for 8 to 10 minutes or until the onions are toasted and golden brown.

Serves 8 to 10

Offer something different from the sliced can-shaped, jellied cranberry sauce this year. This is one of those dishes that will wow your family and guests, and you'll never have to tell them how easy it was.

Combine the cranberry sauce, cranberries, sugar, and orange juice in a medium saucepan, and bring to a boil. Reduce the heat, and simmer for 5 minutes. Remove from the heat, and chill for at least 1 hour before serving.

Serves 6 to 8

1 (14-ounce) can plain jellied cranberry sauce

12 ounces fresh cranberries

1/2 cup sugar

1/2 cup orange juice

— READER RECIPE—

Mom's Punkin Pie Crunch

SANDY HERMAN
PRATTVILLE, ALABAMA

This recipe has been passed down through the generations in Sandy's family. She says it's really more of a cake than a pie, but that her grandmother always called it Punkin Pie Crunch. We all know that grandmothers are always right, so that's what her family continues to call it to this day.

1 (15-ounce) can pumpkin*

1 (12-ounce) can evaporated milk

3 large eggs

1 ½ cups sugar

4 teaspoons pumpkin pie spice

½ teaspoon salt

1 (15 ¼-ounce) box yellow cake mix

1 cup chopped pecans

1 cup (2 sticks) butter, melted

Frozen whipped topping, thawed

Preheat the oven to 350°. Grease a 13 x 9-inch baking dish.

In a large bowl mix the pumpkin, evaporated milk, eggs, sugar, pumpkin pie spice, and salt. Pour the mixture into the baking dish. Sprinkle the dry cake mix over the pumpkin mixture. Top with the pecans, and drizzle with the melted butter. Bake 50 to 55 minutes.

Cool completely and serve with whipped topping.

Serves 8 to 10

* *You'll need to use plain canned pumpkin, not canned pumpkin pie mix, for this recipe.*

PINEAPPLE WALNUT SALAD

A restaurant that we manage to stop at sometimes while on summer vacation serves a salad very much like this. My mom and wife just love the stuff, so they asked me to recreate it for them. They seem pretty happy with the results. It's a cool, crunchy, and creamy dish that is really more dessert than it is salad, but you know we Southerners throw that salad word around quite a bit for things that are obviously not salads. I guess it makes us feel better about eating them.

Drain the pineapple well in a mesh strainer. In a large bowl combine the pineapple, cream cheese, and vanilla. Gently fold in the whipped topping. Stir in the powdered sugar and walnuts. Chill for several hours, and serve cold.

Serves 4 to 6

- 2 (20-ounce) cans crushed pineapple in juice
- 1 (8-ounce) package cream cheese, softened
- 1 teaspoon vanilla extract
- 1 (8-ounce) container frozen whipped topping, thawed
- 1/2 cup powdered sugar
- 1 1/2 cup walnuts, coarsely chopped

My Great Aunt Peggy always makes the Coconut Cake for any family gathering—always. This isn't her recipe, but it comes pretty close. Even if I had her recipe, it wouldn't taste like hers. Isn't food funny that way? It always tastes better when someone else makes it.

FOR THE CAKE:

3 cups all-purpose flour

3 teaspoons baking powder

1/2 teaspoon salt

1 cup (2 sticks) butter, softened

2 1/2 cups sugar

4 large eggs

1 teaspoon vanilla extract

2 teaspoons coconut extract

1 cup milk

1 (6-ounce) package frozen flake grated coconut, thawed

Preheat the oven to 350°. Grease and flour three 8-inch cake pans.

In a large bowl stir the flour, baking powder, and salt together. In another large bowl cream together the butter and sugar with a hand mixer or in a stand mixer. Add the eggs one at a time, mixing well after each one. Add the vanilla and coconut extracts. Alternately add the flour mixture and milk, mixing on low. Once combined, add the thawed coconut and mix well.

Pour the batter into the cake pans, and bake 25 to 30 minutes, or until a toothpick inserted into the center comes out clean. Remove from the pans, and cool completely.

FOR THE ICING:

1/2 cup (1 stick) butter, softened

1 (8-ounce) package cream cheese, softened

1 teaspoon vanilla extract

4 cups powdered sugar

1 cup sweetened flake coconut

In a large bowl combine the butter and cream cheese with an electric mixer or in a stand mixer. Mix in the vanilla, and slowly add the powdered sugar until all has been incorporated.

Once the cakes have cooled, spread the icing in between the layers and on the sides and top of the cake. Once iced, sprinkle sweetened flake coconut on the top and sides.

Serves 6 to 8

Pralines have always been a special treat for me. I can't visit New Orleans without grabbing a few. I just love their caramel flavor, but they can be pretty pricey. Making them at home is easier than you might expect and a lot less expensive.

In a medium saucepan over medium heat, combine the sugars, salt, evaporated milk, and corn syrup, stirring frequently to prevent scorching. Bring to a boil, and cook 6 to 8 minutes or until the mixture reaches the "soft ball" stage or 235° on a candy thermometer.

Remove the pan from the heat, and stir in the pecans, butter, and vanilla extract. Allow to cool for 3 to 5 minutes, stirring occasionally. When the mixture has thickened, but is still pourable, spoon the mixture by the heaping tablespoonsful onto wax paper. Allow to cool completely.

Makes about 2 dozen

- 1 cup white sugar
- 2 cups firmly packed light brown sugar
- 1/4 teaspoon salt
- 3/4 cup evaporated milk
- 2 tablespoons light corn syrup
- 2 cups coarsely chopped pecans
- 3 tablespoons butter
- 2 teaspoons vanilla extract

Pumpkin Pie is synonymous with Thanksgiving. It almost seems impolite to set a Thanksgiving spread without one. The pie is so popular the flavors have made it into other types of food. There are pumpkin pie flavored ice creams, coffees, cheesecakes, and even beer.

1 (15-ounce) can pumpkin*

1 cup sugar

2 eggs

1 teaspoon ground cinnamon

1/2 teaspoon ground nutmeg

1/2 teaspoon salt

1 (8-ounce) can evaporated milk

1/4 cup (1/2 stick) butter, melted

1 (9-inch) deep-dish frozen pie shell, thawed

Preheat the oven to 350°. In a large bowl combine the pumpkin, sugar, eggs, cinnamon, nutmeg, salt, evaporated milk, and butter. Beat with a hand mixer until well blended. Pour into the unbaked pie crust, and bake 35 to 40 minutes or until the center is set.

Serves 6 to 8

* You'll need to use plain canned pumpkin, not canned pumpkin pie mix, for this recipe.

My mom has made these every Christmas for as long as I can remember. Most folks I know have never even heard of them. If you love the chocolate-coated coconut and almond candy bars, I bet you'll enjoy these. They are a real family favorite.

In a large bowl combine the coconut, powdered sugar, butter, sweetened condensed milk, vanilla, and pecans. Work the mixture with your hands until it is well combined. Roll the mixture into 3/4-inch balls, and chill them for at least 30 minutes.

Melt the almond bark using the directions on the package. Using a large fork, dip the chilled balls into the melted chocolate, tapping the fork on the edge of the bowl to remove excess chocolate. Place the coated candies on wax paper to cool.

Makes about 6 dozen

2 cups sweetened flake coconut

8 cups powdered sugar

1/2 cup (1 stick) butter, softened

1 (14-ounce) can sweetened condensed milk

1 teaspoon vanilla extract

4 cups chopped pecans

2 (12-ounce) packages chocolate-flavored almond bark candy coating

Holiday Sugar Cookies

It's become tradition for my son, Jack, and me to make these Christmas cookies every year. I used to be the type of person who strove for perfectly iced sugar cookies. Now I just hand him the icing and let him go. I love that he can do that to me.

2 cups (4 sticks) butter, softened

2 cups sugar

2 large eggs

1 teaspoon vanilla extract

1 teaspoon almond extract

1 teaspoon salt

6 cups all-purpose flour, plus extra for rolling

In a large bowl cream the butter and sugar together until smooth using a hand mixer or in a stand mixer. Add the eggs, vanilla and almond extracts, and salt, and mix well. Add the flour gradually, stirring well after each addition. Cover or wrap the dough tightly, and chill for at least 1 hour, but preferably overnight.

Preheat the oven to 400°. Divide the dough into quarters, and work with one quarter at a time, keeping the other dough refrigerated. Roll the dough out onto a floured surface to about a 1/4-inch thickness. Cut into shapes with your favorite cookie cutters. Transfer cutouts to a cool cookie sheet lined with parchment paper or a silicone baking mat.

Bake 6 to 8 minutes, or until the cookies are set but not browned. Remove from the oven, and allow the cookies to cool on the baking sheet for 7 to 8 minutes. Then transfer them to a cooling rack to cool completely before decorating them.

Makes 4 to 6 dozen cookies depending on the size of the cookie cutter

Most folks are a little intimidated by anything that requires a candy thermometer. I can understand that, but with the right tools, the right recipe, and a little confidence, anyone can make this Peanut Brittle. It's a staple on our holiday table and has been for years.

Butter or spray a large piece of aluminum foil with nonstick cooking spray. In a large cast-iron skillet over medium heat, combine the corn syrup, sugar, and water. Cook until the mixture reaches the "soft ball" stage or 235° on a candy thermometer. Add the peanuts, and stir constantly. Cook until the mixture reaches the "hard crack" stage (300°). The peanuts will start popping, and you might see a little smoke come off the mixture.

Remove from the heat, and quickly add the butter, vanilla, and baking soda. The baking soda will cause the mixture to lighten and foam up. Stir well. Pour the mixture out onto the aluminum foil. Spread thin, and allow to cool completely before breaking into pieces.

Serves 6 to 8

½ cup light corn syrup

1 cup sugar

½ cup water

2 cups raw shelled peanuts

1 teaspoon butter

½ teaspoon vanilla extract

1 teaspoon baking soda

Pecan Log

It's tradition in my family that my grandmother, Nana, makes this every year at Christmas and delivers a log of it to my family, my parents, and my uncle and aunt. It just wouldn't be Christmas without her showing up with the waxed-paper-wrapped Pecan Log. It's easy and oh-so-tasty.

1 (11-ounce) package vanilla wafers

1 (14-ounce) can sweetened condensed milk

3 ½ cups chopped pecans

Crush the vanilla wafers well. In a large bowl combine the crushed wafers, sweetened condensed milk, and pecans. Mix well to combine.

Form into two logs, and wrap each in wax paper. Refrigerate overnight. Slice when ready to serve.

Serves 8 to 10

For many, fudge can be quite an elaborate undertaking. But with this easy, nearly no-fail recipe, anyone can turn out creamy, delicious fudge that is sure to impress. You can add in your favorite nuts (we like walnuts), or you can leave it plain if that's your preference. The recipe works perfectly either way.

Grease an 8 x 8-inch baking dish. In a medium sauce-pan combine the sugar, evaporated milk, and butter, and cook over medium heat until the mixture comes to a boil, stirring frequently. Once it has reached the boiling point, boil for 5 minutes. Stir constantly.

Remove from the heat, and stir in the chocolate chips, vanilla, and marshmallow creme. Stir the ingre-dients until the mixture is creamy and smooth. Pour the mixture into the baking dish. Cool completely, and then cut as desired.

Serves 8 to 10

3 cups sugar

1 (5-ounce) can evaporated milk

3/4 cup (1 1/2 sticks) butter

1 (12-ounce) package chocolate chips

1 teaspoon vanilla extract

1 (7-ounce) jar marshmallow creme

1 cup chopped nuts (optional)

BOURBON BALLS

I can honestly say that I have probably only ever had about three of these in my entire life, though my mother makes them every single Christmas. You see, these are my dad's favorites, and he usually goes and hides them the minute Mom finishes them. He keeps them all to himself, and you'll know why once you try them.

2 cups finely crushed vanilla wafers

2 tablespoons unsweetened cocoa powder

1 cup powdered sugar, plus more for coating

2 tablespoons light corn syrup

1 cup finely chopped pecans

1/2 cup bourbon

In a large bowl combine the crushed vanilla wafers, cocoa powder, 1 cup powdered sugar, corn syrup, and chopped pecans. Add the bourbon, and mix well with your hands. Carefully roll the dough into 1-inch balls, and coat them in powdered sugar. Keep them in a container with a tight-fitting lid.

Makes about 2 dozen

This recipe is surely older than I am. My Nana has made this every year for as long as I can remember. Throw all your preconceived hatred for fruitcake out the window. This recipe is nothing like the traditional, oh-no-let's-re-gift-it fruitcake.

Lightly grease a 13 x 9-inch baking dish. Finely crush the graham crackers. In a large bowl combine the crushed crackers, pecans, chopped cherries, raisins, coconut, marshmallows, and sweetened condensed milk. Mix well. Add the reserved cherry juice by the tablespoon to get the mixture moist and dough-like.

Turn the mixture out into the baking dish, and press flat with your hands. Chill for at least 6 hours, and then cut into bars.

Serves 8 to 10

1 (14.4-ounce) box graham crackers

1 cup pecans, coarsely chopped

1 (10-ounce) jar maraschino cherries, drained and coarsely chopped, reserving juice

1 cup raisins

1 cup sweetened flake coconut, firmly packed

1 ½ cups mini marshmallows

1 (14-ounce) can sweetened condensed milk

Tomato-y Hoppin' John

CRICKETT RUMLEY
LOS ANGELES, CALIFORNIA

Author and screenwriter Crickett Rumley grew up hating black-eyed peas. She would drown them in ketchup to cover the flavor. This recipe is a sophisticated version of her childhood dish. Every time she serves this to folks who claim to share her childhood disdain for the dish, they walk away with changed minds.

1 (16-ounce) package dried black-eyed peas

1 leftover ham bone

6 cups water

1 large onion, cut into wedges

1/2 teaspoon salt (optional)

1 teaspoon black pepper

1 teaspoon crushed red pepper flakes

1 teaspoon dried thyme

2 bay leaves

1 teaspoon minced garlic

1/2 (6-ounce) can tomato paste

1 (14-ounce) can diced tomatoes

Cooked hot white rice

Rinse and sort the peas. Pour them into a large bowl, and cover with water. Allow them to soak overnight or for at least 8 hours.

Drain the peas, and pour them into a large Dutch oven. Add the ham bone, water, onion, salt, black pepper, red pepper, thyme, bay leaves, garlic, tomato paste, and diced tomatoes with the juice. Bring to a boil over medium-high heat, and then reduce the heat to a simmer. Cook about 1 1/2 hours, stirring occasionally, or until the peas are tender.

Remove the ham bone and bay leaves. Cut the remaining meat from the ham bone, and return the meat to the pot. Discard the bone and fat. Serve over white rice.

Serves about 8

Heirloom Bites

FOR MANY, THE SOUTH IS DEFINED BY ITS FOOD. SWEET TEA, OKRA, grits, cornbread, collard greens, red velvet cake, pecan pie—each of these things finds its way onto the unwritten list of foods that are uniquely Southern. I've seen lots written recently about what is and isn't Southern food and about how we should define it. Some say Southern food is about ingredients; other say it's about who cooks it and where it's cooked.

For me, Southern food is about all those things and so much more. Southern food is as much defined by history as it is emotion. Sure, we can automatically classify dishes like gumbo and grits as Southern, but why are those things any more Southern than my Grandmother's pot roast or my mother's stuffed cabbage? There's no need for all this categorization, documentation, or disputation. The truth is, it just doesn't really matter.

What does matter is that you share it, regardless of what you call it. In sharing your food, you share your history, your family, your life. Goodness . . . let's eat.

SOUTHERN FRIED CORN

This is, without a doubt, my most favorite vegetable side dish. Sure, it's a little bit of work, but it is absolutely worth the effort. What really makes this dish is scraping the cob and getting all the remaining starch and milk out of the corn. Though you can replace the bacon grease with more butter, I wouldn't if I were you. It's worth frying the bacon just to get the grease for this recipe.

8 to 10 ears of fresh corn, shucked and washed

2 tablespoons bacon grease (can be replaced with 2 tablespoons butter)

4 tablespoons (½ stick) butter, divided

Salt and black pepper

Place an ear of corn standing up in a large bowl or pan. Run a sharp knife down the cob, cutting the kernels about halfway off but leaving the other half attached. Then turn the knife perpendicular to the cob and scrape down the sides.

Heat a skillet over medium heat, and add the bacon grease and 2 tablespoons of butter. Once the butter has melted, add the corn. Add salt and pepper to taste. Cook 20 to 30 minutes, stirring frequently. Immediately before removing from the heat, add the remaining 2 tablespoons butter and stir until melted. Serve immediately.

Serves 5 to 6

It's important to teach our young folks about where our food comes from, so Jack and I plant a garden every spring. Regardless of what we plant, we always have great success with yellow squash. This is our most favorite way to use our harvest. The bacon in this recipe makes it extra special.

Preheat the oven to 350°. Grease a 13 x 9-inch baking dish.

In a large skillet over medium heat, cook the bacon pieces until just crispy. Add the onions, and cook 7 to 8 minutes or until the onions are translucent. Add the garlic, and cook until fragrant. Add the squash, and cook 10 minutes, stirring occasionally.

Meanwhile, in a large bowl combine the beaten eggs, sour cream, salt, pepper, and cheese. Add the squash and bacon to the bowl, and mix well. Pour the mixture into the baking dish. Top with the crushed crackers, and drizzle with the melted butter. Bake 35 to 40 minutes or until the casserole is browned and bubbly.

Serves 6 to 8

- 5 slices bacon, coarsely chopped
- 1 small onion, finely chopped
- 2 cloves garlic, minced
- 2 pounds ~~yellow summer~~ *zuchini* ~~squash,~~ thinly sliced
- 2 large eggs, beaten
- 1 (8-ounce) container sour cream
- 1/2 teaspoon salt
- 1/8 teaspoon black pepper
- 1 1/2 cups shredded Cheddar cheese
- 1 sleeve buttery round crackers, crushed
- 3 tablespoons butter, melted

My basic recipe for cornbread got thrown out the window the first time I tried this recipe that was Debbie's mother's. I guess, technically, it's more of a hoecake than cornbread, but I just call it delicious. Though there is lots of debate about what true Southern cornbread is, I couldn't care less after having this recipe.

2 tablespoons plus ¹/₂ cup vegetable oil

1 cup self-rising cornmeal

1 ¹/₂ cups self-rising flour

1 large egg

1 ¹/₂ cups milk

Preheat the oven to 400°. Add 2 tablespoons of oil to the bottom of a medium cast-iron skillet. Place the skillet and oil into the oven to heat while you make the batter.

In a large bowl combine the cornmeal, flour, egg, ¹/2 cup oil, and milk. Stir until the ingredients are just combined. Carefully remove the hot skillet from the oven, and pour in the batter. Bake 15 to 17 minutes or until the center springs back when lightly pressed. Turn the oven to broil, and cook until the cornbread is golden brown. Carefully turn the cornbread out onto a plate or platter. Serve immediately.

Serves about 6

COLLARD GREENS WITH HAM HOCKS

My mother loves to tell stories about how I would turn down bowls of ice cream for bowls of collard greens as a kid. I know it sounds crazy, but I guess that just shows my true Southern roots. I still love collard greens.

In a large stockpot combine the water, ham hock, bouillon cubes, salt, and garlic, and then bring the pot to a boil over medium-high heat. Carefully add the collards, and reduce the heat to a low rolling boil. Cover and cook 1 1/2 to 2 hours, stirring occasionally, until the collards are tender.

Serves 6 to 8

- 3 quarts water
- 1 smoked ham hock
- 3 chicken bouillon cubes
- 2 tablespoons salt
- 1 garlic clove
- 2 pounds washed and chopped collard greens

Simple Cucumber and Onion Salad

The simplicity of this easy dish is why I love it so much. The tart and tangy dressing works so well with the cool, crisp cucumber. The problem is whenever I make this, I end up eating so much of it while I'm cooking that I have to make more.

5 or 6 small pickling cucumbers, peeled and sliced

1/2 medium sweet onion, sliced

1/2 cup white vinegar

1/2 cup water

2 teaspoons sugar

1 teaspoon salt

1 garlic clove, finely minced

Add the cucumbers and onions to a large glass or plastic bowl. In a small bowl combine the vinegar, water, sugar, salt, and garlic, and stir until the sugar and salt have dissolved. Pour the dressing over the cucumbers and onions. Refrigerate for at least 1 hour to allow the flavors to blend.

Serves 4 to 5

OLD-FASHIONED BISCUITS

For years I've attempted to master the art of biscuit making the way my mother and grandmother do it. They pour out a big pile of flour right onto the counter, make a well in the middle, mix the ingredients in the middle of the well, and then incorporate their flour. I just can never get them quite right, though. Nonetheless, this is my recipe; it works well and is a little more precise. In the some thirty-odd batches of biscuits it took to arrive at this recipe, one thing I have learned is that the brand of flour you use is important. White Lily® is my favorite brand because the soft winter wheat they use just produces a lighter, flakier biscuit. Any self-rising flour will do; I'm just telling you what I use so your result will be as close to mine as possible.

Preheat the oven to 475°. In a large bowl combine the self-rising flour, salt, and sugar. Add the shortening, and cut it into the flour using a pastry cutter or large fork. The mixture should be crumbly. Stir in the buttermilk until everything is just combined.

Turn the dough out onto a well-floured surface. Knead the dough lightly, being sure to fold the dough in half 3 or 4 times. This helps create flaky layers. Gently roll the dough out to about 3/4-inch thick. Use a biscuit cutter to cut the biscuits by pressing the cutter straight down. Do not twist the cutter. Transfer the biscuits to a baking pan, and lightly brush the tops with 1 tablespoon melted butter. Bake the biscuits for 14 to 16 minutes or until just golden brown. Remove the biscuits from the oven, and brush the tops with the remaining 1 tablespoon melted butter. Serve hot.

Makes 12 to 16 biscuits

- 2 1/2 cups White Lily® self-rising flour
- 1/2 teaspoon salt
- 1 teaspoon sugar
- 1/2 cup vegetable shortening
- 1 cup buttermilk
- 2 tablespoons butter, melted, divided

Okra and Tomatoes

One of the most important things about choosing okra is making sure it's fresh. I prefer the younger, smaller pods. They should be bright green with no dark discoloration, and if you bend back the tip of a pod, it should snap and not be rubbery. You can also use frozen cut okra in the recipe if fresh is not available.

2 tablespoons vegetable oil

1 large onion, chopped

2 cloves garlic, minced

1 pound okra, cut (about 4 cups cut)

1 (14 1/2-ounce) can stewed tomatoes

1 cup chicken broth

Salt and black pepper

Heat the oil in a large skillet over medium heat. Add the onions, and cook 7 to 8 minutes or until the onions are translucent. Add the garlic, and cook 2 minutes. Add the okra, tomatoes with juice, and chicken broth. Bring to a boil, reduce the heat to a simmer, and add salt and pepper to taste. Cover and cook 15 to 20 minutes or until the okra is tender.

Serves about 6

Southern Chocolate Gravy

TINA BUTLER
ROYSE CITY, TEXAS

Who doesn't want an excuse to have chocolate for breakfast? Blogger Tina Butler grew up on it. Her Big Mama always made chocolate gravy for the kids anytime there were biscuits. And though some folks may never have heard of it, it's now a breakfast staple with Tina's kids.

In a medium saucepan over medium heat, whisk together the milk, sugar, flour, and cocoa powder. Bring the mixture to a boil, then reduce the heat to a simmer. Cook until the mixture starts to thicken, stirring constantly. Remove it from the heat, and stir in the butter and vanilla. Serve hot with homemade biscuits.

Serves 4 to 6

- 1 1/4 cups milk
- 2/3 cup sugar
- 2 heaping tablespoons all-purpose flour
- 1 heaping tablespoon unsweetened cocoa powder
- 1 tablespoon butter
- 1/2 teaspoon vanilla extract

The secret ingredient in my Mom's Peach Cobbler is the use of "JIFFY"® Golden Yellow Cake Mix. The mix is a great time saver and gives the cobbler amazing flavor.

Preheat the oven to 350°. Lightly grease a 13 x 9-inch baking dish.

Add the peaches, water, and 1/2 cup sugar to a medium saucepan. Cook over medium-low heat 10 to 15 minutes or until the peaches are soft. Remove from the heat, and drain the peaches, reserving 1/2 cup of the cooking liquid. Place the peaches into the bottom of the baking dish, and add the reserved cooking liquid.

Sprinkle the cake mix over the peaches. Add the remaining 1/4 cup sugar and the cinnamon over the cake mix. Using a butter knife, make swirls in the baking dish to combine some of the dry ingredients with the peach juices below. Drizzle with the melted butter. Bake 30 to 35 minutes or until the top is golden brown and set.

Serves 6 to 8

6 to 7 peaches, peeled and sliced (4 cups sliced)

3 cups water

3/4 cup sugar, divided

1 (9-ounce) box "JIFFY"® Golden Yellow Cake Mix

1/4 teaspoon cinnamon

1/4 cup (1/2 stick) butter, melted

Tomato Tart

This is one of those recipes that looks really impressive, but is actually very easy. This recipe is wonderful with some beautiful heirloom tomatoes. The great thing, too, is that you can adapt this recipe for other uses. I love to make it a mushroom tart by substituting the tomatoes for mushrooms.

1 refrigerated piecrust dough

2 medium ripe tomatoes

1 cup grape or cherry tomatoes

Salt

1 (8-ounce) package cream cheese, softened

2 cloves garlic, minced

1/3 cup grated Parmesan cheese

1/2 teaspoon dried basil or 1 tablespoon of chopped fresh basil

freshly cracked pepper

Preheat the oven to 450°. Bring the piecrust to room temperature, and then unroll it onto a lightly greased cookie sheet. Roll about a 1/4-inch lip around the edge of the piecrust, and pinch it with your fingers to hold it in place. Prick the crust with a fork, and bake 5 minutes. Remove the crust from the oven, and allow it to cool. Lower the oven temperature to 400°.

Slice both sizes of the tomatoes into 1/4-inch thick slices, and place them on paper towels. Salt the tomatoes and allow them to sit for 15 minutes. Blot the tops of the tomatoes with more paper towels to remove excess moisture.

In a small bowl combine the cream cheese, minced garlic, and Parmesan cheese. Spread it over the baked crust. Top with the sliced tomatoes, covering the cream cheese mixture. Sprinkle with the basil and fresh cracked black pepper. Bake 14 to 15 minutes, or until the tart is heated through.

Serves 4 to 6

NANA'S HOOP CHEESE MAC AND CHEESE

Hoop cheese is a farmer's style cheese that commonly has a red or black wax rind. Its popularity is waning for a variety of reasons, but to me it still makes the best macaroni and cheese. As a child, my grandparents both worked in a tiny grocery store that sold hoop cheese. I have such fond memories of my grandmother's mac and cheese and cheese toast using this vintage cheese. If you can't find hoop cheese, a good Cheddar cheese will work just fine.

Bring the water to a boil in a medium saucepan over medium-high heat. Once boiling, add salt and macaroni, and cook until tender. Drain the macaroni, and return it to the pot over low heat. Add the cheese and evaporated milk. Stir until the cheese is melted and creamy. Serve immediately.

Serves about 4

- 1 quart water
- 1 tablespoon salt
- 2 cups dry elbow macaroni
- 3/4 pound red wax hoop cheese, cubed
- 1 (5-ounce) can evaporated milk

PECAN PIE

Quintessentially Southern, this easy Pecan Pie recipe is one of my most favorite desserts and always shows up around Thanksgiving. Most of the time I end up making two just so we have enough to go around.

3 large eggs

1 cup light brown sugar

1 tablespoon all-purpose flour

1 cup light corn syrup

2 tablespoons butter, melted

1 teaspoon vanilla extract

2 cups pecans

1 (9-inch) unbaked frozen pie shell (thawed)

Preheat the oven to 350°. In a medium bowl gently beat the eggs. Stir in the brown sugar and flour. Add the corn syrup, butter, and vanilla, and mix well. Fold in the pecans. Pour the mixture into the unbaked piecrust. Bake 50 to 60 minutes or until set.

Serves 6 to 8

Old—Fashioned Banana Pudding

This Banana Pudding recipe doesn't use a box of pudding mix, but a homemade custard instead. I know it seems like it's just another step, but the packaged stuff just doesn't have the same flavor as homemade. If you don't care for meringue, just top it with some freshly whipped cream when you serve it.

In a medium saucepan over medium-low heat, combine 1 1/2 cups sugar, flour, salt, egg yolks, and milk. Cook the custard, stirring frequently, 15 to 20 minutes or until thickened. Remove the pan from the heat, and add the butter and vanilla. Stir until the butter has melted completely.

Preheat the oven to 325°. Lightly spray a 2 1/2-quart baking dish with nonstick cooking spray. Line the bottom and sides of the dish with vanilla wafers. Slice two bananas on top of the cookies. Then add another layer of cookies, and then two more bananas. Pour the custard over the bananas and cookies.

Whip the egg whites with a hand mixer or in a stand mixer with a whisk attachment until they are frothy. Add the remaining 1/2 cup sugar to the whites. Continue beating until the whites form stiff peaks. Spread evenly over the banana pudding. Bake 12 to 15 minutes or until the tops of the meringue are toasted.

Serves 6 to 8

2 cups sugar, divided
1/2 cup all-purpose flour
Dash of salt
4 large eggs, separated
3 cups milk
1/4 cup (1/2 stick) butter

3 teaspoons vanilla extract
1 (11-ounce) box vanilla
  wafers
4 bananas, sliced

HUMMINGBIRD SHEET CAKE

I love all the flavors of Hummingbird Cake, but I don't always want to tear down the entire kitchen to make an elaborate layer cake. This sheet-cake version packs all that same flavor into a much more simple preparation. The dense and moist cake is truly a Southern dessert staple.

FOR THE CAKE:

3 cups all-purpose flour

2 cups sugar

1 teaspoon salt

1 teaspoon baking soda

1 teaspoon ground cinnamon

3 large eggs, beaten

1 1/2 cups vegetable oil

1 1/2 teaspoons vanilla extract

1 (8-ounce) can crushed pineapple, drained

1 cup chopped pecans

2 bananas, chopped

Preheat the oven to 350°. Lightly grease a 13 x 9-inch baking dish.

In a large bowl combine the flour, sugar, salt, baking soda, and cinnamon, and blend well. Add the eggs and oil, and mix well. Stir in the vanilla, pineapple, pecans, and bananas. Stir gently to combine.

Pour into the baking dish. Bake 40 to 45 minutes or until a toothpick inserted in the center comes out clean. Cool completely.

FOR THE ICING:

1/2 cup (1 stick) butter, softened

1 (8-ounce) package cream cheese, softened

1 teaspoon vanilla extract

4 cups powdered sugar

In a large bowl blend together the butter, cream cheese, and vanilla with a hand mixer or in a stand mixer. Slowly add the powdered sugar until all is incorporated.

Top the cooled cake with the icing. Keep refrigerated.

Serves 8 to 10

RED VELVET CAKE WITH CREAM CHEESE ICING

There isn't a Southern dessert that's more iconic than the Red Velvet Cake. This is the recipe that my family has been using for years. It combines the buttermilk and vinegar that are popular in most recipes and that are credited with giving this cake its signature light, fluffy texture.

Preheat the oven to 350°. Grease and flour two 8-inch cake pans.

In a large bowl mix together the cake flour, salt, and hot chocolate mix. With a mixer, cream the sugar and butter together. Mix in the eggs and vanilla.

In a small bowl mix the buttermilk, vinegar, and baking soda together. Alternately add the flour mixture and the buttermilk mixture to the creamed ingredients until everything has been added. With the mixer on the lowest speed, slowly add the food coloring, and mix until combined.

Divide the batter into the cake pans. Bake 25 to 30 minutes or until a toothpick inserted into the middle comes out clean. Remove from the pans and cool completely.

In a large bowl combine the butter and cream cheese with a hand mixer or in a stand mixer. Mix in the vanilla, and slowly add the powdered sugar. Add the pecans, and mix well.

Once the cakes have cooled, spread the icing in between the layers and on the sides and top of the cake.

Serves 6 to 8

FOR THE CAKE:

2 1/2 cups cake flour

1/2 teaspoon salt

1 package hot chocolate mix (about 3 tablespoons)

1/2 cup (1 stick) butter, softened

2 large eggs

1 1/2 cups sugar

1 teaspoon vanilla extract

1 cup buttermilk

1 tablespoon white vinegar

1 teaspoon baking soda

2 (1-ounce) bottles red food coloring

FOR THE ICING:

1/2 cup (1 stick) butter, softened

1 (8-ounce) package cream cheese, softened

1 teaspoon vanilla extract

4 cups powdered sugar

1 cup coarsely chopped pecans

AMBROSIA FRUIT SALAD

In Greek mythology Ambrosia roughly translates to "food of the gods." But I'm pretty sure the Southern translation means "food of the potluck." You just about can't find a family reunion or church supper south of the Mason-Dixon Line that doesn't have some form of Ambrosia on the table.

1 (15-ounce) can mandarin oranges, drained

1 (15 ½-ounce) can pineapple tidbits, drained

1 (6-ounce) jar maraschino cherries, drained

1 cup sweetened flake coconut

1 cup miniature marshmallows

1 (8-ounce) container frozen whipped topping, thawed

Add the oranges, pineapple, cherries, coconut, and marshmallows to a large bowl. Gently fold in the whipped topping. Refrigerate and serve chilled.

Serves 4 to 6

Linda's Pound Cake

LINDA STUDDARD
WHITE HOUSE, TENNESSEE

This recipe is special to me because it is from one of my most favorite people. Mrs. Studdard is a teacher who had a profound effect on my life. As my teacher, she saw something inside of me that I never knew was there and forced it out. I owe so much of my success to this lady. This cake is just as sweet as she is.

Grease and flour a Bundt pan.

Using a hand mixer or stand mixer, cream together the butter, shortening, and sugar for 5 minutes or until light and fluffy. Add the eggs one at a time, mixing thoroughly after each egg. Add the flour and milk alternately, beginning with 1 cup of flour, then 1/2 cup of milk, 1 cup of flour, 1/2 cup of milk, then 1 cup of flour. Beat well after each addition. Add the almond and vanilla extracts, and mix well. Fill the Bundt pan to within 1 inch of the top.

Place the pan into a cold oven, and turn the oven on to 325°. Bake 1 hour or until the cake pulls away from the sides of the pan and a toothpick inserted into the center comes out clean.

Serves 8 to 10

1 cup (2 sticks) butter, softened
1/2 cup vegetable shortening
3 cups sugar
5 large eggs
3 cups all-purpose flour
1 cup milk
1/2 teaspoon almond extract
1 tablespoon vanilla extract

Milk Syrup

REBECCA PLOKHOOY
HELOTES, TEXAS

This recipe was Rebecca's great-grandmother's and has remained a tightly guarded family secret until now. It's my pleasure to be able to share such a time-honored recipe with the world. I'm sure this stuff would be good on just about anything, but especially on a yummy pound cake (see page 195), with fruit, or even on fresh buttermilk biscuits.

½ cup sugar

1 tablespoon all-purpose flour

1 cup milk

1 teaspoon vanilla extract

In a small saucepan over medium heat, whisk together the sugar, flour, and milk. Bring to a boil, stirring constantly. Remove from the heat, and stir in the vanilla. Serve warm.

Serves 4 to 6

Sweet Bites

In the South, it's nearly impossible to find a proper spread that doesn't include dessert—and most of the time more than one kind. I'll admit I've got a bit of a sweet tooth, so I'm a dessert connoisseur—as my waistline will testify. I've traveled all over the place, and I can say nobody does desserts like the South. When I was growing up, there was never a day in my mother's or grandmother's kitchen when I couldn't find a jar of cookies or a homemade cake under the aluminum lid of a brightly colored cake plate. I think that's the case for most Southern mothers and grandmothers. It might not have always been elaborate, but there was always something sweet. It's just part of Southern culture.

This is one of the first recipes my mother ever made for my son. He sure loves his Gamma, but I'm not sure he doesn't love his Gamma's Chocolate Pie even more. The love that goes into this pie makes it even better. Isn't that the case with most food, though?

Preheat the oven to 400°. Prick the bottom and sides of the thawed piecrust with a fork. Bake the crust 10 to 12 minutes or until the crust is golden brown. Cool completely.

In a medium saucepan combine the butter, 1 cup of sugar, milk, cocoa powder, flour, and egg yolks. Place the pan over medium heat, and heat until boiling, stirring constantly. Reduce the heat to a simmer, and cook until thickened. Remove pan from the heat, and stir in the vanilla. Pour the mixture into the prepared piecrust, and spread evenly.

Make the meringue by whipping the egg whites with a hand mixer or in a stand mixer with a whisk attachment until they are frothy. Add the cream of tartar and the remaining 6 tablespoons of sugar to the whites. Continue beating until the whites form stiff peaks. Spread the meringue evenly over the pie. Bake at 400° 10 to 12 minutes or until the meringue just starts to brown.

Serves 6 to 8

1 (9-inch) frozen prepared piecrust, thawed

3 tablespoons butter

1 cup plus 6 tablespoons sugar, divided

1 cup milk

3 heaping tablespoons unsweetened cocoa powder

3 tablespoons all-purpose flour

3 large eggs, separated

1 teaspoon vanilla extract

Pinch cream of tartar

Pecan Chewies

This recipe represents so much about what The Southern Bite *is. It's one of the first things my wife ever made for me and is one of the first recipes I shared on SouthernBite.com. Everyone who tries these ooey-gooey delicious bar cookies asks for the recipe.*

1 cup (2 sticks) butter, melted

1 cup white sugar

1 cup firmly packed light brown sugar

2 large eggs, well beaten

2 cups self-rising flour

1 cup pecans

2 teaspoons vanilla extract

Preheat the oven to 300°. Grease and flour a 13 x 9-inch baking dish.

In a large bowl stir the butter and sugars together. Add the eggs, and stir well. Add the flour, and stir until all the lumps are gone. Stir in the pecans and vanilla. Spread the mixture into the baking dish. Bake approximately 40 to 50 minutes, being cautious not to overcook. Cool completely before slicing into squares. Store in an airtight container.

Serves 8 to 10

— READER RECIPE —
Strawberry Bread

LESLIE BOWLES
LYMAN, SOUTH CAROLINA

Leslie tells me that she and her husband go strawberry picking every summer as part of their family tradition. This recipe is one of their most favorite ways to use those delicious berries. How great would this be with a big ol' scoop of homemade ice cream? It has me longing for summer.

Preheat the oven to 350°. Grease and flour 2 loaf pans.

In a large bowl mix together the flour, baking powder, salt, cinnamon, and sugar. Stir in the oil, eggs, strawberries, and pecans. Pour the batter into the loaf pans. Bake 1 hour or until the bread is golden brown and a toothpick inserted into the center comes out clean.

Serves 10 to 12

1 cup all-purpose flour

1 teaspoon baking powder

1 teaspoon salt

1 tablespoon ground cinnamon

2 cups sugar

1 1/4 cups vegetable oil

4 large eggs

2 cups coarsely chopped strawberries

1/2 cup chopped pecans

Old-Fashioned Skillet Cake

My wife and friends joke that I'm a simple man because I enjoy recipes with simple flavors. I just love things that are simple and delicious. This recipe, which comes from my great aunt, is just that. Though I never had the chance to meet her, I feel like I know her pretty well each time I make this cake.

2 cups sugar

2 cups self-rising flour

1 ¼ cups milk

2 large eggs

1 teaspoon vanilla extract

¼ cup vegetable oil

Preheat the oven to 350°. In a large bowl combine the sugar, flour, milk, eggs, vanilla, and oil. Mix well. Grease a large, well-seasoned cast-iron skillet. Add the batter to the skillet. Bake 30 to 35 minutes or until golden brown and set. Allow the cake to cool in the pan 15 to 20 minutes before turning the cake out.

Serves 6 to 8

Both of my mother's parents are great cooks. It's odd, though, to find a man of my Papa's age who loves to be in the kitchen like he does. Though he doesn't cook much anymore, if he were to have a signature dish, this would be it. If you cook nothing else in this book, I hope you try this recipe.

Preheat the oven to 325°. Combine the cookie crumbs with the butter. Press the mixture into the bottom and sides of a 9-inch glass pie plate to form the crust.

In a large bowl combine the lemon juice, egg yolks, and sweetened condensed milk. Mix well, and pour into the crust.

Beat the egg whites with a hand mixer or in a stand mixer with the whisk attachment until white and frothy. Add the sugar, and continue beating until stiff peaks form. Spread the meringue on top of the pie filling, being sure to cover the entire pie all the way to the crust.

Bake 15 minutes. Allow to cool to room temperature and then refrigerate. Serve chilled.

Serves 6 to 8

1 1/2 cups crushed vanilla wafers (about 50 cookies)

1/2 cup (1 stick) butter, melted

Juice of 3 lemons

3 large eggs, separated

1 (14-ounce) can sweetened condensed milk

4 tablespoons sugar

Family Jewel Pies

LYNN PETTY
PRATTVILLE, ALABAMA

This is one of those recipes that has been passed down for generations in Lynn's family. She has lots of memories of baking with her mother and grandmother, and one of them is making this pie. It's also one of those recipes that makes an appearance at every family function.

3 (9-inch) frozen piecrusts, thawed

1 (20-ounce) can crushed pineapple in juice

1 (14 1/2-ounce) can red pitted cherries in water, drained

1 1/2 cups sugar

1/2 cup all-purpose flour

1 (3-ounce) box orange-flavored gelatin

5 large bananas, diced

1 cup chopped pecans

Frozen whipped topping, thawed

Preheat the oven to 400°. Prick the bottom and sides of the thawed piecrusts with a fork. Bake the crusts 10 to 12 minutes or until they are golden brown. Cool completely.

Add the pineapple with juice, drained cherries, sugar, flour, and gelatin to a medium saucepan. Heat the mixture over medium heat, and bring to a boil. Remove the pan from the heat, and allow it to cool for about 5 minutes. Then add the bananas and pecans, and stir gently. Pour the mixture into the three baked piecrusts, and refrigerate for at least 3 hours. Serve with whipped topping.

Serves 18 to 24

As a true Southerner, I know that the only way to make great recipes even better is to add either pecans or bacon. In this case both might work, but I'm going to opt for the pecans. This started with my basic chocolate-chip cookie recipe and became something spectacular.

Preheat the oven to 375°. In a large bowl cream the butter and sugars together until combined. Add the eggs and vanilla, and mix well.

In a medium bowl combine the flour, salt, and baking soda. Gradually stir the flour into the butter and sugar mixture. Once the mixtures are combined, stir in the chocolate chips and pecans.

Spoon the dough by heaping tablespoonsful onto an ungreased cookie sheet. Bake 10 to 12 minutes or until the edges are golden brown.

Makes about 4 dozen

1 cup (2 sticks) butter

3/4 cup white sugar

3/4 cup firmly packed light brown sugar

2 large eggs

1 teaspoon vanilla extract

2 1/2 cups all-purpose flour

1 teaspoon salt

1 teaspoon baking soda

2 cups semisweet chocolate chips

1 cup coarsely chopped pecans

KENTUCKY PECAN PIE

This recipe has been passed down through my wife's family for generations. It has all the great flavor of Pecan Pie but with the addition of chocolate. We always serve this pie slightly warm with a big scoop of vanilla ice cream.

1 cup semisweet chocolate chips

1 cup chopped pecans

2 large eggs, beaten

1 cup sugar

1/2 cup (1 stick) butter, melted

1/2 cup all-purpose flour

1 teaspoon vanilla extract

1 (9-inch) deep-dish frozen piecrust, thawed

Preheat the oven to 325°. In a large bowl combine the chocolate chips, pecans, eggs, sugar, butter, flour, and vanilla, and mix well. Pour the mixture into the piecrust, and bake 1 hour. Allow to cool slightly before slicing.

Serves 6 to 8

Sometimes the ease of making brownies and bar cookies like these is what makes them so good. In the case of the recipe, you can have delicious brownies, with all the flavors of Red Velvet Cake, hot from the oven in as little as forty-five minutes.

Preheat the oven to 325°. Grease a 13 x 9-inch baking dish.

In a large bowl combine the cake mix, white chocolate chips, pudding mix, water, oil, eggs, and pecans, and mix well. Spread the mixture into the baking dish. Bake 30 to 35 minutes. Cool completely before slicing.

Serves 8 to 10

- 1 (18 1/4-ounce) box red velvet cake mix
- 1 (12-ounce) bag white chocolate chips
- 1 (3.4-ounce) box vanilla instant pudding mix
- 1/2 cup water
- 1/2 cup vegetable oil
- 2 large eggs
- 1 cup coarsely chopped pecans

APPLE DUMPLINGS

Until I met the Apple Dumpling, I admit I wasn't a huge fan of the texture of cooked apples. I'm not exaggerating when I say that these little babies rock my world. Serve them with some vanilla ice cream, and as my Big Mama used to say, "They'll make your tongue slap your brains out."

1 apple

1 (8-ounce) tube crescent rolls (8-count)

1/2 cup (1 stick) butter, melted

3/4 cup sugar

1/2 teaspoon ground cinnamon

1 1/2 tablespoons all-purpose flour

3/4 cup lemon-lime soda

Whipped cream or vanilla ice cream for serving

Preheat the oven to 350°. Grease an 8 x 8-inch baking dish.

Core and peel the apple, and cut it into eight slices. Open the can of crescent rolls and unroll. Place one apple slice on the wide end of each crescent, and roll it up in the crescent. Place the dumplings into the baking dish.

In a small bowl mix the butter, sugar, cinnamon, and flour until combined. Spoon the mixture over each dumpling.

Pour the lemon-lime soda into the empty spaces in the pan—not over the dumplings. Bake 35 to 40 minutes or until the crescents are golden brown. Serve them warm with fresh whipped cream or vanilla ice cream.

Makes 8 dumplings

Karen's Giant Soft Sugar Cookies

KAREN SIMPSON-NEASBY
LEBANON, MISSOURI

Whether it's a cookie swap at Christmas, Easter family dinner, or just because, this is the recipe that everyone wants Karen to bring. These Giant Soft Sugar Cookies are delicious decorated with your favorite icing and sprinkles or just as yummy with a bowl of fresh berries.

Preheat the oven to 350°. In a large bowl cream together the sugar, butter, and margarine until light and fluffy using a hand mixer or in a stand mixer. Add the eggs one at a time, mixing to incorporate each one afterward. Add the vanilla and almond extracts and butter flavoring.

In another large bowl stir together the flour, baking soda, and cream of tartar. Slowly mix the flour mixture into the creamed ingredients until a very soft dough forms. Drop about 2 tablespoonsful of the dough into a bowl of sugar and roll to coat. Place the dough onto a greased cookie sheet. Continue until all the dough is used. Bake 12 to 15 minutes, and then cool the cookies on a cooling rack.

Makes about 4 dozen, depending on size

- 3 cups sugar
- 1 cup (2 sticks) butter, softened
- 1 cup (2 sticks) margarine, softened
- 6 large eggs
- 2 teaspoons vanilla extract
- 2 teaspoons almond extract
- 2 teaspoons butter flavoring
- 5 cups all-purpose flour
- 2 teaspoons baking soda
- 2 teaspoons cream of tartar
- Sugar for coating

Anytime I see or smell bananas, I'm instantly taken back to my fourth-grade class. Every day, right before lunch, my teacher would go to the closet and retrieve the blackest, nastiest looking banana anyone had ever seen. She seemed to have an endless stash of the things in there. All we kids were mortified by them. But every day she would say, "The darker they are, the sweeter they are." Now, as an adult, I realize the method behind her madness and even prefer bananas a little dark. Bananas that are a little past their prime are always the best ones for banana bread.

1 2/3 cups all-purpose flour

2 teaspoons baking powder

1/2 teaspoon salt

1/4 teaspoon baking soda

3 very ripe bananas

2/3 cup sugar

1/2 cup (1 stick) butter, melted

2 large eggs

1 teaspoon vanilla extract

1 cup chopped pecans

Preheat the oven to 350°. Grease a 9 x 5 x 3-inch loaf pan.

In a large bowl combine the flour, baking powder, salt, and baking soda.

In a medium bowl peel the bananas and mash them well. Stir in the sugar, butter, eggs, and vanilla.

Add the banana mixture to the flour mixture, and then add the pecans. Stir until just combined. Pour the batter into the loaf pan. Bake 45 to 50 minutes or until a toothpick inserted in the center comes out clean.

Serves 6 to 8

Coconut Crunch Pie

VALORIE DEICHMAN
CHAMPAIGN, ILLINOIS

This recipe was made popular by a restaurant in Paducah, Kentucky. It was a favorite of Valorie's mother, and when the business closed in the early 1970s, they gave her the recipe. It quickly became and has remained a must-have at all their family gatherings.

Preheat the oven to 350°. Grease two 9-inch pie dishes.

Using a hand mixer or in a stand mixer, beat the egg whites until they start to stiffen. Gradually add the sugar, and continue beating until stiff peaks form. Add the vanilla, and beat until well mixed. Stir in the graham cracker crumbs, pecans, and coconut. Divide the mixture between the pie dishes. Bake 20 minutes. Allow the pies to cool completely.

When ready to serve, slice the bananas on top of the pies and spread the tops with whipped topping.

Serves 12 to 16

- 8 large egg whites
- 2 cups sugar
- 1 teaspoon vanilla extract
- 2 cups graham cracker crumbs
- 1 cup chopped pecans
- 1 cup sweetened flake coconut
- 4 to 6 bananas
- 1 (16-ounce) container frozen whipped topping, thawed

Skillet Pineapple Upside-Down Cake

The trick to this cake is to make sure you use a very well-seasoned cast-iron skillet. The one I use was my great-grandmother's. There is no telling the thousands of meals that were cooked in that thing. Even though she's no longer with us, using it makes me feel like she's right there in the kitchen with me.

1 cup (2 sticks) butter, divided

1 cup firmly packed light brown sugar

1 (20-ounce) can pineapple slices in juice, reserving juice

1 (15 1/4-ounce) box butter cake mix

3 large eggs

1 (10-ounce) jar maraschino cherries

Preheat the oven to 325°. Add 1/2 cup of butter and the brown sugar to a well-seasoned, medium cast-iron skillet. Place the skillet over medium heat, and stir until the butter is melted. Remove from the heat.

Drain the pineapple juice into a measuring cup, and add enough water to make 1 cup of liquid. Melt the remaining 1/2 cup butter. In a large bowl combine the liquid, cake mix, eggs, and melted butter. Mix well.

Place the drained pineapple rings in the bottom of the skillet on top of the melted butter and sugar mixture. Add the drained cherries in the center of each pineapple ring and other empty spaces if you wish. Pour the cake batter on top of the pineapple and cherries.

Bake 45 to 50 minutes or until a toothpick inserted in the center comes out clean. Immediately cover the pan with a platter and invert to remove the cake from the pan.

Serves 8 to 10

My favorite part of any pound cake is the crusty top part. I've been known to pick off half the top of a cream cheese pound cake (unintentionally, of course) just walking by and picking at it through the day as it sits on the counter. I'm also masterful at slicing everyone's piece of cake and making sure the crusty parts happen to fall on my plate.

1 (8-ounce) package cream cheese, softened

1 1/2 cups (3 sticks) butter, softened

3 cups sugar

1 teaspoon vanilla extract

1 teaspoon almond extract

6 large eggs

1/2 teaspoon salt

3 cups all-purpose flour

Preheat the oven to 300°. Grease and flour a Bundt pan.

In a large bowl cream together the cream cheese and butter with a hand mixer or in a stand mixer. Add the sugar, and beat until light and fluffy. Add the vanilla and almond extracts. Add one egg at a time, mixing after each one.

In a medium bowl mix the salt into the flour. Gradually mix the flour into the batter until combined. Pour the batter into the Bundt pan. Bake 1 hour 25 minutes to 1 hour 35 minutes, or until a toothpick inserted in the center comes out clean. Cool for 15 minutes in the pan; then invert the pan over a serving dish and turn it out.

Serves 8 to 10

Don't worry, Buttermilk Pie doesn't taste anything like buttermilk. It's more of a custard pie. And though it has its origins in the United Kingdom, we like to lay claim to it here down South.

Preheat the oven to 350°. In a large bowl cream the butter and sugar together with a hand mixer or in a stand mixer. Add the eggs, and mix well. Mix in the buttermilk, flour, vanilla, salt, and nutmeg.

Pour the mixture into the unbaked piecrust, and bake 55 minutes to 1 hour, or until set. Allow the pie to cool completely before slicing.

Serves 6 to 8

½ cup (1 stick) butter, softened

2 cups sugar

3 large eggs

1 cup buttermilk

3 heaping tablespoons all-purpose flour

2 teaspoons vanilla extract

Pinch of salt

Dash of ground nutmeg

1 (9-inch) frozen deep dish piecrust, thawed

STRAWBERRY COBBLER

I had never even heard of Strawberry Cobbler until I found the handwritten recipe card in an old cookbook my grandmother had given me. Now it's one of my favorite desserts. It goes great with a big dollop of fresh whipped cream or a scoop of vanilla ice cream—you know, to cut the sweet.

Preheat the oven to 350°. Grease a 2 1/2-quart baking dish.

In a medium pot combine the strawberries, orange juice, and 1/2 cup sugar. Cook over medium heat until the sugar is completely dissolved. Pour the strawberries and liquid into the baking dish.

In a medium bowl combine the flour and remaining 1/2 cup sugar. Cut 1/2 cup butter into the flour with a pastry blender or large fork. Spread on top of the strawberries.

Soften the remaining 1/4 cup butter, and mix it with the brown sugar. Drop the mixture by dollops on top of the flour mixture. Bake 45 to 55 minutes, or until golden and bubbly. Serve with vanilla ice cream.

Serves 6 to 8

- 1 pound fresh strawberries, hulled and sliced
- 3 tablespoons orange juice
- 1 cup sugar, divided
- 1 1/2 cups all-purpose flour
- 3/4 cup butter (1 1/2 sticks), divided
- 1 cup firmly packed light brown sugar
- Vanilla ice cream for serving

Sweet and Salty Toffee Bar Cookies

This isn't a family recipe. This is a Stacey recipe. I don't do it often, but I developed this one just for me. Sure, it's based on a family recipe for chocolate-chip cookies, but I replaced the chocolate chips with chunks of toffee bars because those are my favorite.

1 cup (2 sticks) butter

1 1/2 cups sugar

2 large eggs

1 teaspoon vanilla extract

2 1/2 cups all-purpose flour

1 teaspoon salt

1 teaspoon baking soda

8 (1.4-ounce) chocolate-coated toffee bars, coarsely chopped

Preheat the oven to 375°. In a large bowl cream together the butter and sugar until combined. Add the eggs and vanilla, and mix well.

In a medium bowl combine the flour, salt, and baking soda. Gradually stir the flour into the butter and sugar mixture. Gently fold the chopped toffee bars into the dough.

Spoon the dough by heaping tablespoonsful onto an ungreased cookie sheet. Bake 10 to 12 minutes or until the edges are golden brown.

Makes 4 dozen

Pistachio Puff

LISA KAY SPELL
PALM HARBOR, FLORIDA

As with so many of the reader recipes, this one is a time-honored family favorite for Lisa. Her family has been making this at the holidays for years. While there are many variations on this recipe, this one was her mother's favorite.

In a large bowl combine the whipped topping and pudding mix. Add the pecans, coconut, drained pineapple, drained cherries, and marshmallows, and gently fold to combine. Chill for at least 1 hour before serving.

Serves 4 to 6

- 1 (8-ounce) container frozen whipped topping, thawed
- 1 (3.4-ounce) box instant pistachio pudding mix
- 1 cup finely chopped pecans
- 1 cup sweetened flake coconut
- 1 (20-ounce) can crushed pineapple in juice, drained
- 1 (10-ounce) jar maraschino cherries, drained
- 4 cups miniature marshmallows

CHOCOLATE BAR PIE

Two things make this delicious chocolate pie even better: how easy it is and that it calls for only five ingredients. The filling separates into two distinct layers once it is refrigerated, and the addition of the whipped topping makes three.

2/3 cup milk

4 (1.45-ounce) milk chocolate with almonds candy bars, chopped

20 large marshmallows

1 (16-ounce) container frozen whipped topping, thawed, divided

1 (9-inch) prepared graham cracker piecrust

Pour the milk into a medium saucepan and warm over low heat. Add the chopped chocolate bars, and stir until they are melted. Add the marshmallows and cook, stirring frequently, until the marshmallows are melted. Remove the pan from the heat, and allow the mixture to cool to room temperature. Once cool, stir in about 1 cup of whipped topping and whisk well.

Pour the mixture into the piecrust, and refrigerate overnight to set. Top with the remaining whipped topping and serve.

Serves 6 to 8

Banana Mix-Up

DRU LOVETT
WINFIELD, ALABAMA

Banana pudding was a traditional dish for Dru and her family every Christmas. One Christmas Eve she set out to make it but realized she had no eggs or vanilla wafers. A little ingenuity resulted in this fun dish that has since replaced their traditional banana pudding.

Preheat the oven to 350°. Mix the graham cracker crumbs and butter in a 13 x 9-inch baking dish. Press the mixture flat to create a crust. Bake 10 minutes and cool.

In a large bowl combine the pudding mix and milk. Add the sweetened condensed milk, and mix well. Add half the whipped topping, and mix again. Spread half of the pudding mixture over the cooked, cooled graham cracker crust. Layer the bananas on top of the pudding mixture. Add the remaining pudding mixture, and spread to the edges. Spread the remaining whipped topping on top. Chill at least 1 hour before serving.

Serves 8 to 10

- 3 cups graham cracker crumbs
- 6 tablespoons butter, melted
- 1 (5.1-ounce) package vanilla instant pudding mix
- 2 cups milk
- 1 (14-ounce) can sweetened condensed milk
- 1 (16-ounce) container frozen whipped topping, thawed, divided
- 2 to 3 bananas, sliced

Honeybun Cake

If you love the flavors of the gas station staple, you're sure to love this easy cake. It's great as a dessert, but I really enjoy it for breakfast like its pastry counterpart. Just warm it in the microwave for about ten seconds. It might not be the healthiest breakfast, but it sure is good!

1 (18 ¼-ounce) box yellow cake mix

1 cup (2 sticks) butter, melted

1 (8-ounce) container sour cream

3 large eggs

1 cup firmly packed light brown sugar

2 teaspoons ground cinnamon

2 tablespoons all-purpose flour

2 cups powdered sugar

4 tablespoons milk

1 teaspoon vanilla extract

Preheat the oven to 350°. Grease a 13 x 9-inch baking dish.

In a large bowl combine the cake mix, butter, sour cream, and eggs with a hand mixer or in a stand mixer. Pour half the batter into the baking dish.

In a small bowl combine the brown sugar, cinnamon, and flour. Sprinkle the mixture on top of the batter in the baking dish. Top with the remaining half of the cake batter, and spread to cover. Use a butter knife to make 6 to 8 large swirls in the batter. Bake 40 to 45 minutes or until a toothpick inserted in the center of the cake comes out clean.

In a small bowl make the glaze by combining the powdered sugar, milk, and vanilla. Spread the glaze over the warm cake.

Serves 8 to 10

There's something about the old recipes that get me every time. This recipe is from my wife's great aunt. The simplicity makes them so delicious. Tea Cakes were popular in the South for several reasons, but the main one, I would guess, is because they were inexpensive and fed a crowd. While there are many variations of this recipe, this is my favorite because there's no rolling out dough. It's as simple as mixing the dough and dropping it onto a baking sheet.

Preheat the oven to 350°. In a large bowl stir together the sugar and oil. Once those are combined, add the eggs and vanilla, and mix well. Slowly stir in the self-rising flour. Drop by tablespoonsful onto a greased cookie sheet at least 2 inches apart. Bake 8 to 10 minutes or until the cookies just begin to lightly brown on the edges.

Makes about 2 dozen

1 1/2 cups sugar

1 cup vegetable oil

2 large eggs

2 teaspoons vanilla extract

2 1/2 cups self-rising flour

Hot Milk Sponge Cake

Brandie Skibinski
Salem, Virginia

Everyone remembers those fun little strawberry shortcakes made with the convenient supermarket dessert shells. Well, Brandie has gone and kicked this classic comfort food up a notch. This light, sweet, spongy cake goes perfect with sweet berries and whipped cream on top.

FOR THE TOPPING:

2 pints strawberries

1/4 cup sugar

1 tablespoon lemon juice

Hull the strawberries, and cut them in half. Place the berries in a bowl, and sprinkle them with the sugar and lemon juice. Mix to combine. Cover the bowl, and allow the berries to sit in the refrigerator for about 4 hours. Serve over the Hot Milk Sponge Cake.

Preheat the oven to 350°. Grease a 9 x 9-inch baking dish.

FOR THE CAKE:

1 cup all-purpose flour

1 teaspoon baking powder

2 large eggs

1 cup sugar

1/2 cup milk

2 tablespoons butter

1 teaspoon vanilla extract

In a medium bowl combine the flour and baking powder. In a large bowl beat the eggs on high speed with a hand mixer or in a stand mixer for about 4 minutes or until thick. Gradually add the sugar, and beat on medium for 4 to 5 minutes or until the mixture is fluffy. Add the flour mixture, and mix on low until just combined. Do not overmix.

In a small saucepan over medium heat, add the milk and butter; stir just until the butter is melted. Add the milk and butter mixture to the batter, along with the vanilla. Mix well. Pour the batter into the baking dish, and bake 20 to 25 minutes or until a toothpick inserted in the center comes out clean.

Serves about 6

It just doesn't get much easier than this. I was introduced to these little gems by my childhood friend, Alleda. The best part is that you can use your favorite flavor of cake mix. After trying them all, lemon, chocolate, and strawberry are my favorites.

Preheat the oven to 325°. Lightly grease a cookie sheet.

In a large bowl combine the cake mix, egg, and whipped topping. Place the powdered sugar in a small bowl, and drop tablespoonsful of the cookie batter into the powdered sugar. Roll to coat, and then transfer the coated batter onto the cookie sheet. Bake 13 to 14 minutes.

Makes about 3 dozen

1 (18 1/4-ounce) box cake mix, any flavor

1 large egg

1 (8-ounce) container frozen whipped topping, thawed

1 cup powdered sugar

This is the perfect cool summertime treat. The glossy, silky filling is piled high in a graham cracker crust. I've been eating these pies since I was a child. You can also use frozen limeade concentrate in place of the lemonade for a different flavor.

2 (14-ounce) cans sweetened condensed milk

3 (8-ounce) containers frozen whipped topping, thawed

1 (12-ounce) can frozen lemonade concentrate, thawed

2 prepared graham cracker piecrusts

In a large bowl stir the sweetened condensed milk into the whipped topping by hand. Fold in the lemonade concentrate. Stir gently until the mixture is well combined.

Divide the mixture between the two piecrusts, piling it high in the center. Chill the pies for at least 3 hours.

Serves 12 to 16

Apple Nut Cake

There's just something about this yummy Apple Nut Cake that makes me dream of fall. I can almost hear the crunch of the fallen leaves under my feet. I guess that's because my mom always made this cake in the fall. You're welcome to use whatever type of apples you prefer.

3 cups all-purpose flour

1 teaspoon salt

1 teaspoon baking soda

2 cups sugar

1 ½ cups vegetable oil

2 large eggs

1 teaspoon vanilla extract

3 cups chopped apples (2 to 3 apples)

1 cup chopped pecans

Preheat the oven to 350°. Grease and flour a Bundt pan.

In a large bowl whisk together the flour, salt, and baking soda. Add the sugar, oil, eggs, and vanilla, and mix well. Stir in the apples and pecans.

Pour the batter into the Bundt pan, and bake 1 hour to 1 hour and 10 minutes.

Serves 8 to 10

This recipe comes straight from my grandmother's handwriting. These kinds of recipes that are generations old are my favorites. Just be sure to grease and flour your pan really well, as this one does have a tendency to stick depending on the pan.

Preheat the oven to 325°. Grease and flour a large Bundt pan.

In a large bowl or stand mixer cream together the butter, sugar, and shortening on low speed. Add the eggs one at a time, and beat well.

In another large bowl whisk together the cocoa powder, flour, baking powder, and salt. Add the flour mixture alternately with the milk to the creamed mixture, being sure to blend well after each addition. Add the vanilla extract, and mix well.

Pour the batter into the Bundt pan, and bake 1 hour and 10 minutes or until a toothpick inserted in the middle comes out clean.

Serves 8 to 10

1 cup (2 sticks) butter, softened

3 cups sugar

1/2 cup vegetable shortening

5 large eggs

1/2 cup unsweetened cocoa powder

3 cups all-purpose flour

2 teaspoon baking powder

1/2 teaspoon salt

1 1/4 cups milk

1 teaspoon vanilla extract

Mom's Homemade Banana Ice Cream

TINA KOENIG
SHELTON, CONNECTICUT

Tina's parents were Southerners transplanted to Connecticut. Everyone loved when they would pull out the hand-crank ice-cream maker and whip up their favorite banana ice cream. Tina and her husband have continued the tradition for more than thirty-five years, but they have one rule: To be able to eat it, you have to take a turn at the crank. Sounds like a good deal to me! And while they still make it the old-fashioned way, I'm sure one of those newfangled electric ice cream mixers will work just as well.

8 bananas, peeled and sliced

2 large eggs

1 ½ teaspoons vanilla extract

2 cups sugar

1 (12-ounce) can evaporated milk

1 gallon whole milk

Ice

Rock salt

In a large bowl mash the bananas well. Add the eggs, vanilla, sugar, and evaporated milk, and mix well. Pour the mixture into the canister of a 4-quart ice-cream maker. Add the dasher to the canister, and then pour the whole milk into the canister until about 2 inches remain from the top of the liquid to the top of the canister. Swirl the dasher to mix the ingredients.

Place the lid on the canister, and then place the canister into the tub of the maker. Attach the crank (or motor) to the top. Alternate rock salt and ice around the canister. Turn the crank until the ice cream thickens (or until the motor stops), adding salt and ice around the canister as necessary. Once the mixture has thickened, it can be eaten right away or packed and placed in the freezer to harden more.

Makes about 1 gallon

I know it's easy to just open a brownie mix and add some oil and eggs, but I promise this isn't too much more work. Once you've tried this scratch version, you'll look at those mixes a little differently. This recipe has spoiled my family. They won't even allow me to buy the box mixes anymore.

Preheat the oven to 325°. Grease an 8 x 8-inch baking dish.

In a large bowl combine the butter, sugar, salt, and cocoa powder. Add the vanilla and eggs, and mix well. Stir in the flour, and mix until just combined. Fold in the chocolate chips. Spread the batter into the baking dish, and bake 35 to 40 minutes. Cool completely before cutting.

Serves 8 to 10

3/4 cup (1 1/2 sticks) butter, melted

1 1/2 cups sugar

1/2 teaspoon salt

1/2 cup unsweetened cocoa powder

1 teaspoon vanilla extract

3 large eggs

1 cup all-purpose flour

1/2 cup semisweet chocolate chips

DR PEPPER CAKE

Dr Pepper is my favorite soda and has been for years. So it was natural for me to adapt the usual soda cake to use my favorite beverage. There's something about the cherry flavor in Dr Pepper that works really well in this cake.

FOR THE CAKE:

1 cup (2 sticks) butter

1 1/2 cup mini marshmallows

1/4 cup unsweetened cocoa powder

2 cups all-purpose flour

1 teaspoon baking soda

1 1/2 cups sugar

1 cup Dr Pepper

1/2 cup buttermilk

2 large eggs, slightly beaten

2 teaspoons vanilla extract

Preheat the oven to 350°. Grease a 13 x 9-inch baking pan.

In a medium saucepan over low heat, combine the butter and marshmallows. Cook over medium heat until the marshmallows are melted. Remove the pan from the heat, and stir in the cocoa powder. Set aside.

In a large bowl combine the flour, baking soda, and sugar. Stir together using a large whisk. Add the Dr Pepper, buttermilk, eggs, and vanilla to the flour mixture, and stir until just combined. Slowly add the butter and marshmallow mixture. Stir until combined.

Pour into the baking pan, and bake 30 to 35 minutes or until a toothpick inserted in the center comes out clean.

FOR THE ICING:

1/2 cup (1 stick) butter

1/3 cup Dr Pepper

3 tablespoons unsweetened cocoa powder

1 tablespoon vanilla extract

4 cups powdered sugar

1 cup pecans, coarsely chopped

While the cake bakes, combine the butter, Dr Pepper, and cocoa powder in a medium saucepan over medium-high heat; heat the mixture until it's just boiling. Remove the pan from the heat, and slowly stir in the vanilla and powdered sugar. Spread over the warm cake. Sprinkle with the chopped pecans.

Serves 8 to 10

ACKNOWLEDGMENTS

To Heather, the love of my life, for your support through adversity and your praise in success. I'm so grateful to have you in this "little boat" beside me each day, just paddling along. You're an amazing wife, a remarkable mother, and a loyal friend. I could never thank you enough for all you have done and continue to do—that includes always washing the dishes.

To my son, Jack, for staving off his hunger while Daddy took one more picture of dinner. Within these pages is the food of the generations before you. I hope you will find them as useful as I have and will not only share in the amazing food but also in its connection to your past.

To Laura, for always agreeing to join me on any adventure no matter where it might take us or how much trouble we might get into. God blessed me with a sister; it just took me a few years to meet her.

To Big Mama, for inspiring in me a lifelong passion for food and family. Not a day has passed that I haven't had you in my thoughts. After all this time, I can still feel you in the kitchen with me.

To Christy, for your amazing guidance and support, but mainly for being my friend. If the only opportunity that starting a blog had ever given me was the chance to meet you, I would say it was all well worth it.

To Heather Skelton, my editor, for giving me the opportunity of a lifetime. From our first conversation, I knew that this would be an exciting adventure together. It certainly has been that. There are no words to express how grateful I am to you. I can only hope that you are half as proud of this book as I am.

To Stephanie, Tiffany, and the entire Thomas Nelson team, you all are amazing. I couldn't have wished for a more perfect group of folks to work with.

To Kim, for your willingness to take on the monumental task of bringing my humble recipes to these pages in living color. You have no idea the amount of gratitude my heart holds for your willingness to join me on this journey.

To Ms. Peggi in Texas, for your love and support. You have been a driving force behind the blog and this book. You can never imagine how much I value the relationship we've developed.

To my readers, for your loyalty to my blog, to my family, and to my dream of sharing my food with the world. Without y'all, *The Southern Bite* would be nothing.

ABOUT THE AUTHOR

STACEY LITTLE IS A FOOD BLOGGER WITH A BIG FOLLOWING AND AN even bigger love for Southern food. He grew up refusing bowls of ice cream for bowls of collard greens. From the time he was old enough to bang on pots and pans, Stacey has found himself in the kitchen. He grew up tugging on the apron strings of three of the most influential women in his life--his mother, grandmother, and great-grandmother– and credits much of his success to their love and guidance. Today, his easy, delicious recipes and heartfelt stories have brought millions to his blog, SouthernBite.com, since he created it in 2008. Stacey's deep Southern roots have him firmly planted in central Alabama, where he lives with his wife, little boy, two dogs, and his collection of cast iron skillets.

SouthernBite.com

@southernbite

facebook.com/southernbite

INDEX